Anonymous

Translation of the Provincial and Municipal Laws of Puerto Rico

Anonymous

Translation of the Provincial and Municipal Laws of Puerto Rico

ISBN/EAN: 9783337380427

Printed in Europe, USA, Canada, Australia, Japan

Cover: Foto ©Suzi / pixelio.de

More available books at **www.hansebooks.com**

TRANSLATION

OF THE

PROVINCIAL AND MUNICIPAL LAWS

OF

PUERTO RICO.

DIVISION OF CUSTOMS AND INSULAR AFFAIRS.
WAR DEPARTMENT.
August, 1899.

WASHINGTON:
GOVERNMENT PRINTING OFFICE.
1899.

ROYAL DECREE.

In view of the provisions of the law of March 15, 1895, authorizing my Government to modify the present provincial government of the island of Puerto Rico, according to the prescriptions mentioned in basis second of article 2 of said law, at the suggestion of the secretary of the colonies and with the concurrence of the council of secretaries,

In the name of my august son, the King, Don Alfonso XIII, and as Queen Regent of the Realm,

I decree the following:

ARTICLE 1. The attached provincial law is hereby approved:

ART. 2. The provincial law approved by this decree shall be promulgated and enforced in the island of Puerto Rico.

Given at the Palace on the 31st day of December, 1896.

MARIA CRISTINA.

TOMAS CASTELLANO Y VILLAROYA,
Colonial Secretary.

3

PROVINCIAL LAW APPLIED TO THE ISLAND OF PUERTO RICO.

TITLE I.

THE PROVINCE OF PUERTO RICO AND ITS INHABITANTS.

ARTICLE 1. The territory of the island of Puerto Rico and of the adjacent ones constitutes a province of the Spanish nation, and the city of San Juan Bautista de Puerto Rico is the capital thereof.

For the effects of articles 82 and 84, and according to article 89 of the constitution, it is divided into two regions, which shall be called San Juan and Ponce, in each of which there shall reside a delegate of the Governor-General.

ART. 2. The delegates of the Governor-General shall have the category of chiefs of administration of the second class, and they must possess the necessary requisites to be appointed civil governors in the Peninsula.

They shall enjoy the same salary as the latter and shall perform the duties entrusted to them by this law and the other laws in force in the island of Puerto Rico.

ART. 3. The provisions contained in Title I of the municipal law are applicable to the inhabitants of the province in so far as they refer to their status and rights.

TITLE II.

CIVIL ADMINISTRATION OF THE PROVINCE.

CHAPTER I.—*Provincial authorities.*

ART. 4. The following are the administrative authorities of the province:

1. The Governor-General of the island.
2. The provincial deputation.
3. The provincial committee with the character and duties determined by this law.
4. The delegates of the governor.

ART. 5. The Governor-General and his delegates in the regions are appointed and removed by the Government, as well as all the other employees under their orders.

4

ART. 6. The provincial deputation of the island shall always exercise its duties in full session, and shall be composed of twelve members—that is, six for each region.

They shall remain in office during four years, the corporation being renewed by half every two years by an election which shall take place alternately in the region of San Juan and in that of Ponce.

The provincial deputies shall be elected by the same electors of municipal councils in accordance with the municipal law and in the manner prescribed by the electoral law.

ART. 7. The provincial committee shall be composed of five members appointed in accordance with this law. They shall remain in office for two years.

CHAPTER II.—*Duties of the Governor.*

ART. 8. The Governor-General, and in his place his delegate in the region of San Juan, shall—

1. Preside over the provincial deputation and the committee whenever he is present at their sessions, and shall have a right to vote.

2. Authenticate the minutes of the sessions he may preside over.

3. Communicate and execute the decisions of the deputation and of the committee and see to their exact and punctual fulfillment.

4. Act in the name and represent the province in all its judicial matters, reports, correspondence, and all kinds of communications.

5. Inspect the offices of the province and municipal councils, auditing their cash and other accounts, and examining the archives; see that the laws and general provisions, as well as the decisions, of the deputation are complied with; also see to their execution and prepare all matters it may have to consider. In virtue thereof he shall issue the proper orders, and in cases of omission he shall decide what he may deem best, as well as in cases of negligence or opposition from those charged with their execution, informing the supreme goverment of all these matters.

6. Suspend the decisions of the provincial deputation and of the municipal councils when it is proper according to this law and to the municipal law, and exercise the powers which the same and the other laws in force grant him.

7. Suspend from their offices the provincial deputies, mayors, deputy mayors, and aldermen in the cases and manner prescribed by this law and by the municipal law.

8. Supplement the provincial and municipal action either by appointing the deputation and municipal councils whenever they do not meet, or completing their number whenever they do not meet in a sufficient number to adopt resolutions, or supplementing the duties of the same corporations should they refuse to execute them, submitting the matter to the colonial secretary after a report from the council of administration.

ART. 9. The deputation shall adopt resolutions on all matters submitted by the Governor-General.

ART. 10. The delegates of the Governor-General shall very carefully see that public order is preserved within the territory of their corre-. sponding region, for which purpose the military authorities shall give them their assistance whenever they request it.

ART. 11. The Governor-General shall designate the person who is to substitute the delegates during their absence or sickness.

ART. 12. The office of delegate of the Governor-General is incompatible with every other provincial or municipal office of any kind whatsoever, without prejudice to the provisions of the preceding article.

CHAPTER III.—*Organization and mode of procedure of the provincial deputation.*

ART. 13. The procedure for the election of provincial deputies shall be subject to the provisions of the electoral law.

ART. 14. All persons having the necessary requisites to be deputies to the Cortes and who reside within the province may be provincial deputies.

The following can not be provincial deputies in any case whatsoever:

1. Deputies to the Cortes.
2. Mayors, deputy mayors, and aldermen.
3. Employees of the State, province, or municipality holding office.
4. All persons directly or indirectly interested in services, contracts, or the furnishing of supplies within the province and for account of the same, of the State or of the municipal councils.
5. All persons holding public offices which by special laws are declared incompatible with that of provincial deputy.
6. All persons engaged in administrative or judicial litigation with the deputation or with the establishment subject to and under the administration of the same.

The same persons to whom this right is granted may excuse themselves from holding the offices of councilors, according to article 43 of the municipal law.

ART. 15. The election of provincial deputies shall take place during the first fifteen days of the month of September.

ART. 16. The deputies elected shall present their certificates of election in the office of the secretary of the deputation eight days before that on which the sessions are to begin. On this day, without previous call, the deputies who may have presented their certificates shall meet under the chairmanship of the Governor-General or his delegate and shall proceed to the temporary organization of the deputation.

ART. 17. The provincial deputation shall be temporarily organized under the chairmanship of the oldest member, and the two youngest amongst those present shall act as secretaries.

ART. 18. After the deputation has been temporarily organized, and during the same session, it shall elect two committees, each composed of three members; the first committee shall investigate the certificates already presented and those that may be subsequently presented by the interested parties; the second committee shall investigate the certificates of the members composing the former. Both committees shall immediately present their reports to the provincial deputation, which, in view thereof, shall proceed instantly to approve, in a proper case, the certificates and the legal capacity of the elected members, and decide on all claims and protests arising from the election, as well as all questions in reference to its own organization in accordance with the laws.

An appeal lies to the territorial audiencia of the island against these decisions of the provincial deputation.

ART. 19. After the certificates against which there is no protest affecting the legality of the election are approved, and in order to definitely organize itself, the deputation shall proceed to elect from amongst its members a president, a vice-president, and two secretaries to act as such at all the sessions to be held until its renewal.

ART. 20. The deputies who may not have presented their certificates for the final organization shall be considered as having renounced the office.

The deputation shall declare the vacancy and communicate the same to the Governor-General, who shall order a partial election to be held at the time and in the manner prescribed by law.

ART. 21. Should the deputation order the annullment of a certificate, it shall communicate its decision to the Governor-General, who shall immediately order its publication in the Gaceta.

ART. 22. This decision shall be final, and in consequence thereof the partial election shall be held, if the interested party does not appeal from it within eight, days to the audiencia of the territory.

ART. 23. The provincial deputation shall meet only in the capital of the province every year on the first working day of the months of April and November.

ART. 24. The first session of each period shall be inaugurated by the Governor-General or his delegate in San Juan, in the name of the government.

ART. 25. The office of deputy is without compensation, honorary and subject to liability, and can not be renounced after having been accepted except for just cause.

ART. 26. The extraordinary vacancies occurring for any reason whatsoever shall be filled by partial election, whenever an ordinary session of the deputation is to be held before the general renewal.

When a vacancy occurs by reason of administrative or judicial suspension, or after the period above-mentioned, the Governor-General shall temporarily fill it with any person who may have already held the office of provincial deputy by election.

The person appointed shall continue to hold the office until the suspension of the deputy whose place he is filling is finally decided upon, or until the first renewal should the former discontinue on account of the series established.

ART. 27. In case of permanent removal, the first renewal shall take place two years thereafter, those representing the first region discontinuing their tenure of office, namely, at the first ordinary election to be held after the lapse of said period of time.

ART. 28. The provincial deputation shall have the power to accept or refuse resignations and to declare vacancies in accordance with the provisions of this law.

The Governor-General shall order ordinary and extraordinary elections whenever they are to be held according to law and in the manner prescribed by the same.

The elections shall be announced within the five days following that on which they were decided upon, and shall take place within a period not less than fifteen days nor more than thirty after the call.

ART. 29. The deputation shall determine at its first session of each semiannual period the number of sessions it shall hold during the same. Should it be necessary, it may order an adjournment.

Should any causes arise during sessions which should render their continuance dangerous, the Governor-General may suspend or adjourn them immediately, notifying the Government of his action.

ART. 30. The deputation shall meet in extraordinary session whenever in the opinion of the Governor-General he considers it necessary to take action on any special question.

ART. 31. The Governor-General shall issue a call notifying in writing and at his domicile each one of the members eight days beforehand, stating the object of the session, if an extraordinary one is in question. The session shall be advertised in the *Gaceta de Puerto Rico* the same period in advance.

ART. 32. When the Governor-General considers on account of special reasons that public order may be endangered if an extraordinary session takes place, he shall suspend the call.

ART. 33. The sessions of the provincial deputation shall be public, except in the cases when for special reasons it is advisable that they be secret.

An extract of the minutes of the sessions shall be published in the *Gaceta de Puerto Rico.*

ART. 34. Attendance at the sessions is obligatory. Any deputy who, without a legitimate and justifiable reason, does not comply with the provisions of this article, shall incur a fine of twenty-five pesetas for each offence, being, moreover, liable for any damages arising from his tardiness.

Any deputy who shall find it necessary to absent himself shall notify the delegate of the Governor-General; otherwise he shall incur the liabilities mentioned in the preceding paragraph.

During the sessions permission from the deputation is required to obtain leave of absence, which shall only be granted in so far as its effects do not conflict with the provisions of the following article.

ART. 35. In order to deliberate on any subject the presence of an absolute majority of the total number of deputies is necessary.

ART. 36. In order to adopt a resolution the vote of the majority of the members present is necessary, except as provided for in a contrary case by this law. In case of a tie, voting shall be resumed the following day, and should there be a second tie, the president shall cast the deciding vote.

ART. 37. The provisions of articles 62, 63, 104, 108, 110, 112, 113, and 116 of the municipal law are applicable to the provincial deputations in so far as possible.

ART. 38. For the dispatch of business, order of sessions, and mode of procedure the deputation shall draft the regulations to be observed.

ART. 39. At each one of the semiannual meetings the president and secretaries of the deputation shall submit a statement mentioning the business it has to consider, with a notice of all pending matters, state of the accounts, funds, and provincial administration.

CHAPTER IV.—*Jurisdiction and powers of the provincial deputation.*

ART. 40. The administration and direction of the special interests of the province are under the jurisdiction of the provincial deputation, in so far as they do not appertain to the municipal boards, according to this law and the municipal law, and particularly in all that refers to the following subjects:

1. The drafting and approving every year the budgets with sufficient funds to attend to the services entrusted to it.

2. The examination and, in a proper case, the approval of the accounts of the provincial budget, which shall be presented every year by the section of local administration, declaring the administrative liabilities resulting therefrom.

3. The establishment and preservation of the services devoted to the comfort of the inhabitants of the province and the development of their material and moral interests.

4. The resolution in accordance with the laws and regulations of everything it may deem convenient for the administration in the island of public works, postal and telegraphic, maritime and land communications, of agriculture, industry, commerce, immigration and colonization, public instruction, charities and health, fairs, expositions, and other institutions for improvement and other similar purposes, without prejudice to the high inspection and the inherent powers of sovereignty which the laws reserve to the Government of the nation.

5. The administration of provincial funds, either for the use, enjoyment and preservation of all kinds of property, acts, and rights belonging to the province or to the establishments depending on the same, or for the settlement, distribution, investment, and account of the

necessary revenues to carry into execution the services intrusted to the deputation.

6. The decision without further appeal of the questions referring to the organization of municipal corporations, claims and protests in the elections of councilors, incidents of the same, capacity of the members elected and excuses of the same, in the cases and manner provided for by the municipal and electoral laws.

7. The resolution, without further appeal, of the questions relating to the constitution of municipalities, the addition to and survey of municipal districts.

8. The fulfillment of the duties which the municipal law assigns to the same, and all the others intrusted to them by special laws.

The deputation shall comply with the laws and provisions issued for their execution in all matters which, according to the present law, do not come under its exclusive jurisdiction and wherein it has to act by delegation.

ART. 41. The provisions of article 78 of the municipal law are applicable to the provincial deputation in all that appertains to the nature of the services entrusted to this corporation.

ART. 42. The deputation shall, moreover, have all the powers conferred on the same by the municipal law as well as all those conferred by other special laws.

ART. 43. The resolutions adopted by the provincial deputation, in conformity with the provisions of article 40, are final, without prejudice to the appeals established by this law.

ART. 44. The Governor-General shall suspend, of his own accord or at the instance of any resident of the province, the execution of the resolutions of the provincial deputation whenever he considers them contrary to the laws or the general interests of the nation and shall temporarily adopt, of his own accord, the rulings required by public necessities which might be abandoned by reason of the suspension, submitting the matter to the colonial secretary, after a report from the council of administration.

ART. 45. The resolutions of the provincial deputation shall be communicated on or before the third day to the Governor-General for the effects of the preceding article.

The suspension shall be communicated to the provincial deputation within the eight days following the notification of the resolution, after which period it is final by its own right.

The period shall begin from the time when the proceedings were received, in case the governor called for them in order to examine the same.

The suspension, in any case, shall state the reasons therefor, and a definite and precise statement shall be made of the legal provisions on which it is based.

ART. 46. After the suspension has been communicated, the provincial deputation may appeal to the colonial secretary, to whom the Governor-General shall forward the appeal with the record of the proceedings and his report by the first mail.

The colonial secretary shall decide without loss of time after consultation with the council of state.

ART. 47. The governor shall also suspend the execution of the resolutions of the provincial deputation whenever injury may result to the civil rights of a third person.

In this case the suspension shall only take place when the interested party so requests it, presenting at the same time a complaint against the resolution.

The governor shall order the suspension, if it should be in order, within the three days following that on which the petition was presented, and shall immediately notify the interested party.

ART. 48. Any person considering himself injured in his civil rights by the resolutions of the deputation, whether their execution has been suspended or otherwise, by virtue of the provisions of the preceding articles, may object by means of a complaint to the proper judge or court, in accordance with the laws.

The judge or court taking cognizance of the matter may suspend, by means of a first ruling and on the request of the party interested, the execution of the resolution appealed from, should this not have taken place in conformity with Article 46, whenever he considers it proper and convenient in order to avoid serious and irretrievable injury.

A period of thirty days is granted for the presentation of this complaint, beginning from the date of the notice of the resolution, or from the date in which the suspension was communicated in a proper case; should this period of time elapse without the complaint having been presented, the suspension shall cease by right and the resolution accepted.

ART. 49. When a resolution is suspended or appealed from by virtue of the provisions of the preceding articles, the Governor-General shall forward by the first mail the data to the colonial secretary in the first case, or to the proper judge or court within the period of eight days in the second case.

The colonial secretary shall decide in the manner prescribed by article 46.

ART. 50. Should a resolution of the provincial deputation injure the rights of private individuals, those having contributed with their vote to the adoption of the same shall be held liable for indemnity or restitution to the injured party before the proper courts.

ART. 51. The municipal councils may appeal within the period of eight days, counting from that of the publication or notice of the assessment, against all kinds of assessments, approved in accordance with the provisions of the municipal law, which the deputation may order amongst the towns of the province in order to cover the general and necessary expenses for the provincial requirements.

After this period has elapsed it shall be final without further remedy.

The Governor-General shall decide on the appeal after hearing the council of administration, and his confirmatory ruling may give occasion to an appeal to the court of the island hearing administrative litigation.

CHAPTER V.—*Organization and mode of procedure of the provincial committee.*

ART. 52. The provincial deputation shall appoint, from amongst its members, the members of the provincial committee and its vice-president.

ART. 53. The extraordinary vacancies of the provincial committee shall be filled in the same manner as prescribed in the preceding article, and those appointed shall occupy, in regard to the series of cessation (salida), the place of the members they substitute.

ART. 54. The provincial committee shall have the powers granted to the same by this law; it is always in session and resides in the capital of the province.

ART. 55. The provincial committee shall meet as often as required by the business entrusted to it, in accordance with the order fixed in the first session of each month.

ART. 56. The delegate of the Governor-General in San Juan de Puerto Rico is the president of the committee, and the secretary of the deputation shall be the secretary without a vote.

ART. 57. In order to deliberate on any subject the presence of three members is necessary, and this number of favorable votes is necessary for the adoption of a resolution.

When this number of favorable votes is not obtained at a ballot, voting shall be resumed the following day, and the decision of the majority shall cause the resolution to be adopted; should there still be a tie the vote of the president shall be the deciding one.

ART. 58. After the office has been accepted, attendance at the sessions is obligatory.

When a member does not attend four consecutive sessions without permission from the committee or just cause accepted by the same, it shall be understood that he renounces his office, without prejudice to the liability he may have incurred according to article 34.

ART. 59. The sessions of the committee shall be public, except in the cases when it should be decided to hold secret ones for special reasons.

ART. 60. The provisions of article 37 are applicable to these sessions in so far as they are compatible with the organization and mode of procedure of this body.

CHAPTER VI.—*Jurisdiction and powers of the provincial committee.*

ART. 61. The provincial committee shall have the following powers:

1. As a consulting body, to give its opinion whenever the rules and regulations prescribe it and whenever the Governor-General, of his

own accord, or by command of the Government, deems convenient to request it.

' 2. To temporarily take charge of the business intrusted to the provincial deputation, when by reason of the urgency or the nature of the matter the meeting of the same can not be awaited; in such cases the provincial deputies who are at the capital at the time must attend the sessions. The deputation, at its first meeting, shall decide whatever it may deem convenient in order to reach a final resolution.

ART. 62. The competencies of jurisdiction and powers between the administrative and judicial authorities shall be decided in accordance with the laws.

ART. 63. The Governor-General shall direct the litigation instituted in the name of the province.

In order to institute ordinary complaints of greater amount the resolution of the provincial deputation is necessary; in all other cases that of the Governor-General is sufficient, after hearing the committee.

CHAPTER VII.—*Employees and agents of the provincial administration.*

ART. 64. The following are the divisions of the provincial deputation:
1. Office of the secretary.
2. Office of the auditor.
3. Office of the treasurer.

There shall be a chief at the head of each of these divisions, under whose orders all the necessary employees shall serve.

ART. 65. The personnel, the salary, and the duties of all the employees of said divisions, and the regulations for the interior management, shall be prescribed by the deputation.

ART. 66. The deputation appoints and removes all its employees.

ART. 67. The Governor-General may also remove or suspend the secretary, auditor, and treasurer for a serious reason, justified by proceedings.

The suspension can not exceed a period of four months.

ART. 68. The interested parties may enter complaints against the ruling of removal or suspension before the colonial secretary through the governor, who by the first mail shall forward the appeal with the record of the proceedings and his report thereon.

The colonial secretary shall decide without loss of time and without further appeal, after hearing the council of state.

ART. 69. The provincial deputation may appoint anyone of its members or employees to inspect the municipal councils in order to ascertain the condition of its services and archives.

During these visits no rulings shall be issued concerning municipal matters, and the delegates shall confine themselves to informing the deputation, which in view thereof shall adopt the proper resolutions in conformity with this law.

ART. 70. The secretary is intrusted with the preparation and dispatch of the matters of which the committee and the deputation have to take cognizance, with the drafting of its minutes and resolutions, the correspondence, and the care and preservation of the archives.

He shall sign, with the president, the opinions and resolutions of the committee and of the deputation, and shall authorize them with the seal of the province, the care of which is intrusted to him, and shall also see that the proper parties are duly notified.

ART. 71. The treasurer is the only person intrusted with the custody of the provincial funds, and as such he shall give the bond which the deputation may require.

CHAPTER VIII.—Budgets and provincial accounts.

ART. 72. The provincial deputation shall follow in the accounting of its funds the provisions of the decree of September 12 and the instructions of October 4, 1870, issued for the management of the financial administration and accounting system of the colonies, and the others in force relating to special services.

ART. 73. The provincial deputation shall forward every year its ' budgets to the Governor-General three months before the commencement of the fiscal year, for the double purpose of correcting the legal extralimitations, should there be any, and to prevent the general interests of the nation from suffering.

ART. 74. The deputation may appeal from the decisions of the Governor-General, presenting the same to the Governor himself in order that he may forward it to the colonial secretary, who shall decide thereon without loss of time, after hearing the council of state.

If no resolution has been reached by the colonial secretary fifteen days before the commencement of the fiscal year, the budgets approved by the deputation shall be in force.

ART. 75. The general disbursing office appertains to the president of the deputation or to whomsoever represents him whilst the deputation is in session; when it is not in session it shall appertain to the vice-president of the provincial committee.

ART. 76. The monthly distribution of funds shall appertain to the deputation, or if it should not be in session to the associate committee of the deputies who may be in the capital.

ART. 77. The provincial budget shall precisely include the necessary amounts, in accordance with the revenues of the province, to cover the following services:

1. Personnel and supplies of its offices and divisions.

2. Preservation and management of the buildings and estates belonging to the province.

3. Establishment and preservation of those the object of which is the comfort of the inhabitants of the province.

4. Public works, telegraphic and postal, land and maritime communications, agriculture, industry and commerce, immigration and colonization, public instruction, charities and sanitation.

5. Subscription to the Gaceta de Madrid and that of Puerto Rico.

6. Fund for emergencies and public calamities.

7. Advertisements, printing, and other expenses which may be considered necessary or convenient.

8. All the other expenses which may be clearly and precisely required by this and by other laws in the part to be complied with by the province.

ART. 78. The vote of an absolute majority of the total number of deputies is necessary for the approval of the budget. If the budget should not be approved at the beginning of the fiscal year, the previous budget shall remain in force in its necessary parts, or in a proper case the provisions of article 74 shall be observed.

ART. 79. In order to cover the expenditures specified in the provincial budget, the deputation shall use as receipts or revenues:

1. The income and product of the property belonging to the province and to the establishments and institutions the government and direction of which appertains to the provincial deputation.

2. The penalties authorized by law and enacted by the deputation, on the taxes and imposts of the State, the collection of which is intrusted to the general intendance of the Treasury.

3. The assessment which for the balance shall be assigned to the municipalities as a provincial proportion, in relation to what each one pays as direct taxation and to the entity of the corresponding budgets.

ART. 80. This proportion shall be included in the budget of each town, and its entire amount shall be paid in the treasurer's office at the time of the ordinary collection, or before should the municipal councils voluntarily make the payment thereof.

ART. 81. The provisions of articles 165, 166, 169, 170, and 178 of the municipal law are applicable to the deputation in all that appertains to the collection, management, and custody of the provincial funds.

ART. 82. The deputation shall audit, and in a proper case approve, the accounts of the provincial budget, which shall be made and submitted every year by the section of local administration.

TITLE III.

DEPENDENCY AND LIABILITY OF DEPUTIES AND AGENTS OF THE PROVINCIAL ADMINISTRATION.

ART. 83. The provincial deputation and the committee are subject to the proper administrative liability in all matters that do not come under their jurisdiction, in conformity with the laws.

The Governor-General, as the superior chief of all the authorities of the island, shall execute all the resolutions of the deputation of a final character, and it is his duty to forward to the same and to the committee the laws, provisions, and instructions communicated to him by the colonial secretary, in all that concerns them.

The section of local administration in the general government and by delegation of the same shall have in charge for this purpose the services paid for from the provincial budget and the accounting system in reference thereto, and shall be liable for the nonobservance of the laws and of the legitimate resolutions of the deputation.

ART. 84. The provincial deputation shall be liable:

1. By reason of manifest infraction of the law in its actions or resolutions, whether it be on account of its having transcended its powers or abused those appertaining to it.

2. By reason of disobedience to the supreme Government or to the Governor-General in the matters in which it acts by delegation and under orders from them.

3. By disrespect to the authority.

4. By reason of negligence or carelessness causing injury to the interests or services intrusted to it.

ART. 85. The liability shall be demanded administratively or judicially, in a proper case, according to the nature of the act or omission.

The liability shall only be demanded from the deputies who incurred the omission or took a direct part in the act or resolution which caused it.

ART. 86. The administrative liability includes the warning, fine, and suspension which it is the duty of the Governor-General to impose.

The provisions of article 191 of the municipal law are applicable to these penalties.

ART. 87. The following rules shall be borne in mind for the imposition or exaction of fines:

1. The determination of the amount appertains to the Governor-General.

2. The fines shall not exceed 500 pesetas.

3. The fines imposed on the deputies can not be paid from the provincial funds.

4. The provisions of articles 194, 195, and 196 of the municipal law are applicable to these fines.

ART. 88. Suspension is in order in the cases stated in article 199 of the municipal law.

The provisions of articles 200, 201, and 204 of the municipal law are applicable to the proceedings for the suspension of provincial deputies.

The provisions of article 203 of the municipal law shall be observed should criminal liability exist.

ART. 89. The Governor-General, after hearing the board of authorities, may suspend the deputation, or, without that requisite, he may order of his own accord the suspension of its members, provided there remains a sufficient number of them to deliberate:

1. When the deputation or any of its members exceeds the limit of its legitimate faculties with injury to the governmental or judicial authority or endangering public order.

2. By reason of delinquency.

In the first case he shall immediately notify the Government, in order that the latter may raise the suspension or order the removal, by reason of the resolutions adopted by the council of secretaries, within the period of two months counted from the date on which the first direct steamer leaves for the Peninsula, after the lapse of which without either ruling the suspension shall be raised by reason of right. In the second case the proper courts shall immediately take cognizance of the matter, and whatever these may decide shall be carried into execution, not only in regard to the suspension but also to the final liabilities.

ART. 90. Any deputy who has been removed from office can not be reelected until six years at least have elapsed, unless the sentence does not impose a penalty of disqualification for a longer period.

ART. 91. The audiencia of the territory shall be the competent court in first instance, with the appeals to the supreme court authorized by the laws, in the offenses committed by the deputation in a body and by the provincial deputies in the exercise of their functions.

ART. 92. The employees and agents of the provincial administration appointed by the deputation shall render obedience to the same and are liable to it in accordance with this law.

ART. 93. The Governor-General and the colonial secretary in the proper cases, shall exercise the high inspection over all the services of the island, in whatsoever manner they may be rendered, in accordance with the faculties inherent to the sovereignty reserved by the laws to the government of the nation.

ADDITIONAL PROVISIONS.

1. All former laws and provisions relative to the provincial government of the island of Puerto Rico are hereby repealed.

2. The laws, decrees, royal orders, and regulations in force in the Peninsula deciding concrete points of the provincial administration, or which are a complement or developments unforeseen by this law, shall govern as supplementary legislation in so far as they may be applied to the special case in question, and in the lack of a legal precept or governmental provision issued to the contrary for the island of Puerto Rico.

3. The Government shall draft, in accordance with this law, the necessary provisions for the execution of the same.

Madrid, December 31, 1896.

Approved by Her Majesty.

CASTELLANO.

ROYAL DECREE.

In view of the provisions of the law of March 15, 1895, which authorizes my Government to modify the municipal régime in force in the island of Puerto Rico in accordance with the conditions established in basis 1 of article 2 of said law, at the suggestion of the Colonial Secretary, in concurrence with the council of secretaries,

In the name of my august son the King, Don Alfonso XIII, and as Queen Regent of the Realm,

I decree the following:

ARTICLE 1. The annexed municipal law is approved.

ART. 2. The municipal law approved by this decree shall be promulgated and enforced in the island of Puerto Rico.

Given at the Palace on December 31, 1896.

MARIA CRISTINA.

TOMAS CASTELLANO Y VILLARROYA,
Colonial Secretary.

18

MUNICIPAL LAW APPLIED TO THE ISLAND OF PUERTO RICO.

TITLE I.

MUNICIPAL DISTRICTS AND THEIR INHABITANTS.

CHAPTER I.—*Municipal districts and their alterations.*

ARTICLE 1. A municipality is the legal association of all the persons who reside in a municipal district.

ART. 2. A municipal district is the territory under the administrative jurisdiction of a municipal council.

The following are the requisites of a municipal district:

1. That the number of residing inhabitants is not less than 2,000.

2. That it has or that there may be apportioned to it a territory in proportion to its population.

3. That it can meet the obligatory municipal expenses with the income authorized by law.

The present municipal districts which have a municipal council may continue in existence, even though they do not fill the requisite prescribed in number 1 of this article, until otherwise ordered by the Government.

ART. 3. Municipal districts may be changed—

1. By the absorption in whole to one or more adjoining districts.

2. By the separation of part of a district, either to constitute with the same or with one or more parts an independent municipality, or either to add it to one or to several of the adjoining districts.

3. In order to change from one town to another the seat of a district.

ART. 4. The abolition of a municipality and its absorption into one or more of the adjoining ones is proper—

1. When on account of the lack of means or other good reasons it is resolved and requested by the municipal councils and a majority of the inhabitants of the municipalities interested.

2. When on account of the widening and development of building, the limits of the towns become confused and it is not easy to determine their true limits.

ART. 5. The separation of a part of a district in order to add it to other existing ones is proper when requested by a majority of the residents of the portion to be separated and when it can be effected without prejudicing the legitimate interests of the rest of the municipality nor cause it to lose the conditions mentioned in article 2.

The separation of part of a district in order to constitute one or more independent municipalities, in itself or in union with one or more portions of adjoining districts, may take place by the agreement and on the request of a majority of the persons interested and without prejudicing legitimate interests of other towns, provided the new districts which are to be formed include the conditions mentioned in article 2.

ART. 6. In any of the cases of addition or separation the persons interested shall indicate the new demarcations of lands and shall effect the division of property, lands owned in common, public uses and credits, without prejudice to the rights of ownership and public and private servitudes existing.

ART. 7. The questions relating to the constitution of municipalities and to the addition and survey of districts shall be decided without further appeal, except that of complaint, by the provincial deputation.

ART. 8. Every municipal district shall form part of a judicial district of the province, and can not belong, for any reason whatsoever, to different jurisdictions of the same order.

ART. 9. In order to transfer a municipal district from one to another judicial district, as well as to transfer the seat from one town to another, proceedings shall be instituted which shall be decided by the provincial deputation without further appeal, except that of complaint, hearing the municipal councils of the town and of the seats of the judicial district, as well as the territorial audiencia.

ART. 10. Groups of population, although they have their own municipal council, situated at a maximum distance of five kilometers from the district line of the capital of the island or from any other town containing the same or a larger number of inhabitants, may be added to said districts by virtue of a resolution of the provincial deputation.

CHAPTER II.—*Inhabitants of municipal districts.*

ART. 11. The inhabitants of a municipal district are divided into residents and transients.

The residents are subdivided into residents and denizens.

ART. 12. Residents are all emancipated Spaniards who permanently reside in a municipal district and are recorded as such in the register of the town.

Denizens are all Spaniards who, without being emancipated, reside permanently within the district, forming part of the family or household of a resident.

As emancipated for all the effects of this law are considered all Spaniards who have reached the age of twenty-five years.

Transients are all persons who are not included in the foregoing paragraphs and are temporarily in the district.

ART. 13. Every Spaniard must be registered as a resident or denizen of some municipality.

A person who resides alternately in different ones shall claim the residence of one of them.

Nobody can be a resident of more than one town; if any person is recorded in the registry of two or more towns, the last declared residence shall be considered the valid one, the previous ones being thenceforth considered annulled.

ART. 14. The character of resident is declared officially, or at the instance of a party, by the respective municipal council.

ART. 15. The municipal council shall officially declare as residents all emancipated Spaniards who at the time of the formation or correction of the registry have resided continuously for two years in the municipal district.

A similar declaration shall be made with regard to the persons who are filling public offices at that time requiring a fixed residence in the district, even though they have not completed the two years.

ART. 16. The municipal council, any time of the year, shall declare every person who requests it a resident, said person not being thereby exempted from paying the municipal taxes which correspond to him up to that date in the town of his previous residence.

The petitioner must prove that he has resided continuously in the district for a period of six months at least.

CHAPTER III.—*Registration.*

ART. 17. It is the duty of municipal councils to make a register of all the inhabitants of their district, stating whether they are residents, denizens, or transients, name, age, status (whether married or single), profession, residence, and other details required by statistics.

ART. 18. Every five years a new register shall be made, which shall be corrected every intermediate year by the official entries or at the instance of a party and by the eliminations on account of legal incapacity, death, or transfers of residence which have taken place during the year.

Residents who change their domicile, the parents and guardians of those who become incapacitated, and the heirs or legatees of deceased persons are obliged to make the proper report to the municipal council, in order that the elimination may take place.

The delegates of the Governor-General shall take care that the municipal councils rectify the registry of residents periodically.

ART. 19. After the five-yearly registration has been made, or its annual rectification, the municipal council shall make up two lists in abstract, one stating the changes which have taken place during the year and another including all the inhabitants there may be in the district at the conclusion of the work.

These lists shall be published at once.

ART. 20. The registration and the rectifications shall take place in the month of December, and shall be, as well as the lists, at the disposal of all those who wish to examine them in the office of the secretary of the municipal council on working days and during office hours.

In the fifteen following days the municipal council shall receive the complaints which any resident of the district may make against the registry or its rectifications, and shall decide thereon during the rest of the month, entering in the book of minutes the decision adopted with regard to each person interested, who shall immediately be informed thereof in writing.

ART. 21. Against these decisions of the municipal councils an appeal may be taken to the provincial deputation.

The appeal shall be instituted before the mayor within the three days following the written notification of the decision.

The mayor shall forward, without any delay whatever, the proceedings to the provincial deputation.

The deputation within the period of one month shall decide, without further appeal, in view of the reasons alleged by the persons interested and the municipal council, and shall communicate to the latter its sentence, with the reasons therefor, after which, the proper corrections having been made during the following weeks, the registration shall be declared terminated and the corrected lists shall be published.

ART. 22. The register is a solemn, public, and authentic document, which shall serve for all administrative purposes.

ART. 23. The municipal councils shall forward to the provincial deputation, in the last month of each fiscal year, a statement of the number of residents, denizens, and transients, classified as may be determined by the Governor-General of the island, for the census of the population.

The delegates of the Governor-General shall see to the exact fulfillment of this service.

CHAPTER IV.—*Rights and obligations of inhabitants of municipal districts.*

ART. 24. All the inhabitants of a municipal district have a right of action against the decisions of municipal councils, as well as to denounce and prosecute criminally mayors, aldermen, and members of the assembly of associates in the cases, and at the time and in the manner prescribed by the provisions of this law and those of the royal decree and regulations of September 12, 1868.

ART. 25. All persons appealing to the municipal authority have a right to demand of the same a statement, in which there shall be stated the claim or complaint and the date and hour on which it was made.

ART. 26. All the residents of a municipal district have a share in the lands owned in common or benefits of a communal character, as well as in the rights of general interest granted the association, and are subject to the taxes which may be imposed for the municipal and provincial services, in the manner and proportion determined by this law.

If the town has property owned by the community, the following rules shall be observed for its annual arrangement and distribution:

1. When the property in common can not be equally utilized by all the residents of a town, the enjoyment and benefit shall be awarded at public auction among the said residents exclusively, after the necessary appraisements and its division into lots in a proper case.

2. If the property is susceptible of general utilization, the municipal council shall distribute the products among all the residents, distributing them for the purpose into divisions or lots, which shall be awarded to each person in accordance with any of the three following bases:

By families or residents.

By persons or inhabitants.

By the quota of assessment, should there be any.

3. The distribution, according to residents, shall be made with strict equality to each one of them, without regard to the number of persons their family may consist of or of the number who live with them and under their dependence.

The distribution by persons shall take place by allotting to each resident the portion corresponding to him in proportion to the number of resident inhabitants of which their household or family consists.

The distribution according to the quota of assessment shall take place among the residents subject to the payment thereof, and awarding to each person the part corresponding in proportion to the quota allotted. In such case, there shall be awarded to the poor residents exempted from the payment, a portion not exceeding that which corresponds to the taxpayer paying the lowest quota.

4. In extraordinary cases, and when the requirements of the town necessitate it, the municipal council may order the auction of the so-called lands owned in common among the residents, or fix the price which each one is to pay for the lot which may have been awarded to him.

The administration, use, and preservation of municipal timber lands shall be subject to the forestry laws in force in Puerto Rico.

ART. 27. In so far as the municipal financial administration is concerned, as well as the rights and obligations arising therefrom with regard to residents, the following shall be considered as owners of the estates they cultivate, occupy, or administer:

1. The administrators, attorneys, or agents of nonresident owners, without prejudice to the following cases, be they either at the head of an agricultural, industrial, or commercial establishment opened in the district for the account and in the name of the latter, or if they limit themselves to the collection of rents.

2. Farmers, lessees, or coproprietors of rural estates, whether the owners or administrators reside in the district or not.

3. Tenants of town property, when the same is leased to one person only, and its owner, administrator, or agent does not reside in the district.

ART. 28. Foreigners shall enjoy the rights granted them by the treaties or laws in force.

TITLE II.

GOVERNMENT AND ORGANIZATION OF MUNICIPALITIES.

CHAPTER I.—*Municipal councils and municipal boards.*

ART. 29. In each district there shall be a municipal council and a municipal board.

ART. 30. The government and interior administration of each municipal district is under the jurisdiction of the municipal councils and municipal boards, in accordance with the laws.

ART. 31. The municipal council is composed of councilors divided into three categories—mayor, deputy mayors, and aldermen. They shall be elected by the residents of the municipal district who have electoral rights, in the manner fixed by law.

ART. 32. The municipal councils have the double character of juridical entities and of administrative authorities.

Their duty as juridical entities is:

1. To legally represent municipalities.

2. To preserve all property and to defend the rights and interests belonging to the same, including those which are peculiar to those towns which, preserving their private administration, have intrusted the same to the municipal board authorized by this law.

ART. 33. In their character of administrative authorities, municipal councils shall exercise jurisdiction over the entire municipal district or the territory to which their action extends, in the manner and form determined by the laws.

ART. 34. The budgets shall be drafted by the municipal councils and approved by the municipal boards.

ART. 35. It is the duty of municipal boards to establish and create means to obtain funds, at the time and in the manner ordered by this law, as well as to revise and audit the accounts of municipal councils.

CHAPTER II.—*Organization of municipal councils.*

ART. 36. The census of the population shall determine the number of councilors corresponding to each municipality and their distribution as deputy mayors and aldermen; the number of deputies shall determine the number of municipal subdistricts each district is to be divided into, and the number of residents in each one of said subdistricts shall determine the number of wards and the number of electoral districts.

ART. 37. The municipal councils shall arrange the territorial division in such manner that representation of minorities in municipal corporations is facilitated.

ART. 38. Each subdistrict shall be divided into wards when, on account of the number of its inhabitants or on account of local circumstances, it is thus required for the good of the municipal service.

Each ward shall be included within one subdistrict.

All suburbs removed from the limits of the town, as well as any other part of the municipal district removed from the said limits, shall constitute a ward.

In each ward there shall be a mayor (alcalde) of the same appointed from among the voters permanently residing in the ward.

The mayor may freely remove mayors of wards.

ART. 39. In the towns referred to in chapter 2 of title 3 of this law, the duties of mayor of a ward shall be discharged by the presidents of the boards who must be elected as prescribed in the same chapter; and they can not be removed except for the reasons mentioned in this law for deputy mayors.

ART. 40. The first division of the district into subdistricts, wards, and electoral districts shall be made in accordance with the following rules:

1. The municipal council shall order the division and shall have it published in the *Gaceta de Puerto Rico* and in the local newspapers, should there be any, or by means of edicts otherwise.

2. The residents and denizens of the district may within the following month, to be counted from the date of the publication of the resolution, make such complaints against the same as they may consider proper.

3. Should there be no objection, the resolution shall be considered as final at the end of the period mentioned above; should there be any, the municipal council shall investigate them and forward the same, with its report, together with a certified copy of the resolution of division, to the provincial deputation within the fifteen days following the expiration of the period.

4. The provincial deputation shall examine the data and the objections, and shall decide what may be proper with regard to the points referred to in the latter, and shall communicate its report within one month from the date of the reception of the proceedings.

ART. 41. After the division of a municipal district has been made, in accordance with the prescriptions of this law, it can not be changed until two years at least have elapsed, and only in case time shows that it does not correspond to the conditions and circumstances above mentioned, and never in the three months preceding any ordinary election.

The proceedings for change shall be instituted on the initiative of the municipal council and shall pursue the same course as those mentioned in the foregoing article.

ART. 42. The number of councilors which each electoral district is to elect and the number each elector may vote for, as well as the formation of electoral lists, shall be governed by the provisions of the electoral law.

ART. 43. The following can in no case be councilors:

1. Provincial deputies or deputies to the Cortes, and senators.

2. Municipal judges, notaries, and other persons who fill public

offices which have been declared incompatible with the office of councilor by special laws.

3. Those who discharge public remunerated functions, even though
they have renounced the salary.

4. Those who directly or indirectly are interested in services, contracts, or furnishing of supplies within the municipal district for the
account of their municipal council, of the province or State.

5. Debtors as taxpayers to the municipal, provincial, or general
funds, who have been judicially notified.

6. Those who have an administrative or judicial suit pending with
the municipal council, or with the establishments under its dependency
or administration.

Relationship between councilors is not a cause of incapacity.

In order to discharge the duties of deputy mayor or syndic, it is
necessary to know how to read and write.

The following may excuse themselves from acting as councilors:

1. Persons over sixty years of age and those physically incapacitated.

2. Persons who have been senators, deputies to the Cortes, provincial deputies, and councilors for two years after having ceased in their
respective offices.

Councilors shall cease in their offices if they should at any time not
possess all the conditions mentioned in this law.

Each electoral district shall appoint the number of councilors which
belongs to the same in proportion to the number of electors.

ART. 44. Municipal elections shall be held in the first two weeks of
the month of May.

ART. 55. The municipal councils shall be renewed by half every
two years, the oldest councilors in service going out at each renewal.

In cases of ordinary or extraordinary renewals, the election of the
councilors shall be made by the same electoral districts which elected
the departing ones.

ART. 46. A partial election shall be held when, at least six months
before the ordinary elections, vacancies occur which amount to a third
of the total number of councilors.

If the vacancies occur after said period and amount to the number
indicated, they shall be temporarily filled, until the first ordinary election, by the persons whom the Governor-General may appoint from
among those who had formerly been elected to the municipal council.

ART. 47. The municipal councils shall make a report of the aforesaid
vacancies to the Governor-General, who, within ten days exactly, shall
order the election held within a period not less than fifteen nor more
than twenty days, counted from the time the resolution is communicated to the respective municipal council.

ART. 48. For the purposes of this law, in so far as the series of cessation is concerned, the persons elected shall, in cases of vacancies, be
considered as the councilors they have substituted.

ART. 49. The municipal councils shall meet on the first day of the fiscal year—that is, on the first of July—after an ordinary election has been held, the departing councilors ceasing on that day and the persons elected taking possession.

The latter shall present their certificates and credentials issued by the board of general examination in the office of the secretary of the municipal council three days at least before the meeting is to be held. Persons who do not comply with this requisite, or are not present on the day fixed for the establishment of the corporation, without giving good reasons for their absence, shall incur the fine which shall be fixed by the delegate of the Governor-General.

The councilors elect who repeat this offence and cause thereby that the corporation can not establish itself on the day fixed for the purpose and for which they have been cited, shall incur double the fine above mentioned.

ART. 50. If for any reason whatsoever the new municipal council has not been named by the first day of the first month of the fiscal year, the departing councilors shall be replaced by temporary ones appointed in accordance with the provisions of the second paragraph of article 46.

ART. 51. The departing mayor shall be present at the act of the installation of the new municipal council, in order to receive the councilors elect and install them in their offices, and shall immediately thereafter retire with the departing councilors.

ART. 52. The mayors shall be appointed from among the councilors by the Governor-General or by the municipal councils.

When the Governor-General makes use of the privilege mentioned the person he appoints shall be the mayor.

During the time the Governor-General does not deem it proper to appoint a mayor, the person elected by the municipal corporation shall hold that office.

The Governor-General may also remove mayors when he considers that there is good cause therefor, hearing the council of administration.

ART. 53. Mayors shall receive the salary which is fixed for them in the municipal budget, provided there is no deficit in the latter, and it is thus ordered by the municipal council.

ART. 54. Deputy mayors shall be appointed in the same manner as mayors. The Governor-General may order their removal and replacement by other councilors.

ART. 55. When vacancies occur in the office of mayor or deputy mayors within the half year preceding the ordinary elections, the vacancies shall be filled as follows: Those of mayors, if the Governor-General does not make use of his privilege to appoint them, by the deputies, and those of the latter by the councilors who obtained the highest number of votes or are older, in cases of ties.

ART. 56. The mayors shall present themselves, without loss of time, before the municipal council assembled for the purpose, and shall receive possession from the retiring mayor or from the person who is temporarily filling the office.

ART. 57. When the municipal corporation is to be installed, the mayor shall call them for that purpose and shall install the deputy mayors and councilors. The president and the members of the former municipal council shall be present at this ceremony to receive the new councilors, and shall retire after the latter are installed in office.

ART. 58. After the new municipal council has been established under the presidency of the mayor appointed by the Governor-General, or by the person who obtained the highest number of votes in a proper case, shall proceed to the election of advocate syndics, and in a proper case to the election of deputy mayors.

The advocate-syndics (procuradores sindicos) represent the corporation in all the suits which may be instituted in the defence of the municipal interests, and shall revise and audit all the local accounts and budgets.

The ballots shall be secret and the votes shall be written on slips of paper, which shall be deposited in a box; and separate ones shall be held for mayors and syndics, those who obtain the highest absolute majority of the total number of members present being elected.

If no absolute majority is obtained, the corporation shall continue established as it is, balloting being resumed on the following day, those who receive a relative majority being proclaimed. In cases of ties, it shall be decided by lot.

ART. 59. Immediately after the persons elected take possession, the municipal council shall fix the days and hours on which ordinary sessions are to be held, with which the inaugural session shall be closed. One ordinary session shall be held each week at least.

ART. 60. On the same day the mayor shall appoint, from among the electors, the mayors of wards. The persons appointed shall hold office until the next renewal of the municipal council, if they are not removed before by the mayor.

ART. 61. The mayor shall report to the municipal corporation in the next session the appointments of mayors of wards referred to in the foregoing article.

ART. 62. In the second session the municipal council shall fix the number of permanent committees into which it is to be divided, entrusting to each one of them the general business of one or more of the branches which the law places in their charge, and determining the number of members which are to compose the same.

After coming to a decision, the election of the members thereof shall immediately be proceeded with in secret ballot and with slips of paper, those who obtain the highest number of votes being elected, ties being decided by lot.

ART. 63. During the course of the year the municipal council may appoint, when it considers it advisable, special committees, which shall be elected in the same manner as the permanent ones, but they shall be discontinued when the commission entrusted to them is concluded.

When a deputy mayor or syndic is elected to a committee he shall be its president.

ART. 64. The councilors and the members of the board of associate members may be reelected.

They shall cease to be such if they incur any of the incompatibilities established.

ART. 65. The office of deputy mayor, syndic, councilor, associate member, and mayor of a ward are without compensation, obligatory and honorary.

The mayors, the deputies, and the mayors of wards shall use as a symbol of their authority the insignia established by the regulations.

The deputy mayors and aldermen shall not have any special title as such.

ART. 66. The questions relative to the incidents of elections, capacity of the persons elected, and other similar ones shall be decided without further appeal, except by complaint, by the provincial deputation.

CHAPTER III.—*The organization of the municipal board.*

ART. 67. The municipal boards shall be composed of the municipal council and of the associate members in equal number to councilors appointed from among the taxpayers of the subdistrict.

ART. 68. For this purpose all residents may be appointed who are obliged to contribute a quota to the municipal expenses, and where no quota is assessed those who pay a land tax or an industrial, commercial, or professional one.

· Persons who do not have the capacity to be councilors are excepted, however, as well as those who are such at the present time, their associates, and their relatives within the fourth degree, and the employees and clerks of the municipal council.

In towns which do not have over 2,000 inhabitants the exclusion by reason of relationship shall be limited to the second degree.

ART. 69. The appointment shall be made by lot among the taxpayers, divided into sections, in accordance with the following rules:

1. The number of sections shall be determined in one of the first four sessions of the year by each municipal council, taking into consideration the population of the town and the amount and class of wealth of the same, and shall in no case be less than a third part of the councilors.

2. In each section there shall be included the residents or landowners whose professions or trade are more or less related to each other, in accordance with the groupings and classifications made for the payment of direct taxes, in such manner that the members of one taxpaying class do not form part of different sections. Residents who pay taxes for more than one purpose, or are included in two or more industries, shall enter the section they may select.

3. In towns where it is not possible to make any distinction of classes, the payment of taxes of its inhabitants being made for the same reason or in which there are no industrial branches of sufficient importance to require the formation of a special section, the assessment of the latter shall be made by streets, wards, or parishes.

The same shall be done when any of the sections formed according to the foregoing rule is so large that it in itself constitutes the fourth part of the associate members of the municipal board.

4. To each section there shall be assigned the number of members or associates which correspond to the same in proportion to the amount of tax paid by all its members.

ART. 70. The municipal council, before the end of the first month of each fiscal year, shall publish the result of the formation of sections, against which any of the persons interested may complain within the period of eight days to the provincial deputation.

The deputation must decide within the following fifteen days, and its decision shall be final for the two subsequent years.

ART. 71. After the formation of sections has thus taken place, the municipal council in a public session shall announce it two days in advance in the ordinary manner, and at least one hour before on the said day shall proceed with the sortition of the associate members to the sections and shall have the result immediately published.

The board must be definitely established within the second month of the fiscal year.

The persons elected shall fill their office for the entire respective fiscal year.

ART. 72. The municipal council shall admit and decide within the period of eight days all excuses or objections, making a new sortition if it is proper, without prejudice to the appeal for review to the provincial deputation.

ART. 73. When a vacancy occurs in the number of associate members a new sortition shall take place, with the formalities mentioned in article 71, in order that their number may always be complete.

TITLE III.

MUNICIPAL ADMINISTRATION.

CHAPTER I.—*Powers of municipal councils.*

ART. 74. Municipal councils are financial administrative corporations, and may only exercise the functions entrusted to them by the laws.

Their title is impersonal.

ART. 75. The government and administration of the private interests of towns is under the jurisdiction of municipal councils, subject to the laws, and particularly in all that refers to the following subjects:

First. Establishment and creation of municipal services referring to the arrangement and ornamentation of public roads, comfort and hygiene of the neighborhood, encouragement of its material and moral interests, and security of persons and property, as follows:

1. Opening and survey of streets and parks and of all kinds of roads of communication.
2. Paving, lighting, and sewerage.
3. Water supply.
4. Promenades and trees.
5. Bathing establishments, laundries, market houses, and slaughterhouses.
6. Fairs and markets.
7. Institutions for instruction and sanitary services.
8. Municipal buildings and in general all kinds of public works necessary for the fulfillment of the services subject to the special legislation on public works.
9. Surveillance and police.

Second. Urban and rural police—that is, all that refers to the good order and surveillance of the established municipal services, care of public roads in general, cleanliness, hygiene, and health of the town.

Third. Municipal administration, which includes the use, care, and preservation of all estates, property, and rights belonging to the municipality, and to the establishments depending therefrom, and the determination, distribution, collection, investment, and account of all receipts and imposts necessary for the execution of the municipal services.

ART. 76. Municipal councils are specially obliged, under the personal liability imputable to all councilors guilty of negligence or omission, to prevent all kinds of trespasses on property and to administratively recover recent usurpations of rights of the community, recent usurpations being understood those the possession of which has not covered a longer period than one year and a day.

After the one year and a day mentioned have elapsed, the payment of the expenses caused by the recovery by any other legal procedure shall be for the account of the negligent councilors.

ART. 77. It is the obligation of municipal councils to construct and keep in repair municipal roads. In so far as the rural roads are concerned, the municipal councils shall oblige the persons interested in the same to preserve and repair them.

In order to attain these objects the proper measures with regard to municipal roads shall be adopted by the board of associates, and with regard to the rural roads by a board of the persons interested.

The provincial deputation shall see to the fulfillment of this part of the administration by virtue of the powers granted the same by the laws.

ART. 78. It is the duty of municipal councils to procure, alone or with the assistance of the members, in the manner hereafter expressed, an exact compliance, in accordance with the means and necessities of the town, of the purposes and services which, according to the present law, are intrusted to their action and surveillance, and particularly the following:

1. Preservation and repair of public roads.
2. Rural and city police.
3. Police for security.
4. Primary instruction.
5. Administration, custody, and preservation of all estates, property, and rights of the town.
6. Charitable institutions.

Municipal resolutions relating to fairs and markets, surveillance, police, and security, primary instruction and charitable institutions require the previous approval of the provincial deputation.

In matters which do not come under their jurisdiction, they are also obliged to assist the action of the general and local authorities in the fulfillment of that part of the laws which refers to the inhabitants of the municipal district, or which are to be complied with within the same, for which purpose they shall proceed in accordance with the prescriptions of the said laws and the regulations issued for their execution.

ART. 79. For the fulfillment of the obligations of municipal councils, the following are their special powers:

1. Establishment of the municipal ordinances for the city and rural police.
2. The appointment of its employees and agents in all branches in accordance with this law and other special ones.

The agents of municipal surveillance who carry arms shall depend exclusively on the mayor with regard to their appointment and removal.

3. The establishment of personal services.

ART. 80. The municipal ordinances for the rural and town police which may be issued by the municipal councils for the government of their respective districts, shall be submitted to the approval of the Governor-General, after a report from the provincial deputation.

The decision of the Governor-General shall be final when it is in accordance with the report of the provincial deputation.

In case of disagreement the proceedings shall be submitted to the colonial secretary, who shall decide, hearing the council of state.

ART. 81. Any infractions of the ordinances and regulations shall be punished by fines not to exceed 50 pesetas in the capital of a province and in towns having an equal number of population; 25 in seats of judicial districts and towns of 4,000 inhabitants, and 15 in other towns, with reparation for the damage done and indemnification for costs, and arrest of one day for each peso in cases of insolvency.

For the collection of fines the proceedings shall be in accordance with articles 194 (rules 1, 2, and 3), 195, and 197.

The municipal judge shall discharge the duties entrusted by article 97 to the judge of first instance.

Against an administrative decision the person fined may appeal to the municipal council and institute the proceedings referred to in article 196, in a proper case.

ART. 82. The appointment and removal of all the employees and clerks paid with municipal funds shall be made by the municipal councils.

Officials destined to professional services shall have the qualifications and fill the conditions determined in the laws relating to the same.

ART. 83. Personal services are inforced in order to assist in the construction of municipal public works of all kinds; municipal councils have the power to require the same of all inhabitants over sixteen years of age and under fifty, with the exception of those taken care of in charitable institutions, soldiers in active service, and persons incapacitated for work.

The number of days shall not exceed twenty per year nor ten consecutive ones, each day redeemable by the person interested at the rate of pay given laborers in the locality.

With the exception of the public works mentioned in this article, no personal services of any kind can be required, the mayor or deputy mayor requiring them incurring liability.

ART. 84. The municipal councils, with the authority and approval of the provincial deputation, may form by themselves and with the adjoining ones associations and communities for the construction and preservation of roads, rural police, care of property owned in common, and other subjects of their exclusive interest. These communities shall be governed by a board composed of one delegate for each municipal council, presided over by the member elected by the board.

The board shall draw up the accounts and budgets, which shall be submitted to the municipal boards of each town, and should they not be approved by all or by any of them the provincial deputation shall decide.

ART. 85. The communities of municipal councils shall always be voluntary and shall be governed by boards of delegates of the same, which shall alternately meet in the respective seats of the municipal associated subdistricts.

Whenever any complaints are made against the administration of said communities they shall be decided by the provincial deputation, with the exception of questions of ownership, which are reserved to the courts of justice.

ART. 86. Municipal councils may represent, in so far as matters of their competency are concerned, the provincial deputation, the delegate of the Governor-General, the Governor-General, the Government, and the Cortes.

Except when they make complaints against the mayor, they must do

4080——3

so through the same. When they address themselves to the Government or to the Cortes, they shall do so through the Governor-General.

If within a period of eight days the proper authorities do not take action on representations of municipal councils (excepting the Governor-General), said councils may repeat the same in the shape of a direct complaint.

If within a period of two months the Governor-General does not take action upon representations of municipal councils, the latter may repeat the same directly, in the shape of a complaint, addressed to the colonial secretary or to the Cortes in a proper case.

ART. 87. All the resolutions of municipal councils in questions of their competency are final, with the exception of the appeals determined by the laws.

ART. 88. Resolutions regarding pruning and cutting of timber in municipal forests require the approval of the provincial deputation, subject to the laws relating to the matter and those referring to the reform and abolition of municipal establishments for charity and instruction.

ART. 89. Alienations and exchanges of municipal property shall be made in accordance with the following rules:

1. Lands remaining over from public roads and granted to private ownership and useless objects may be exclusively sold by the municipal council.

2. Contracts relating to municipal establishments of no use for the service to which they had been destined, and private credits in favor of the people, as well as all contracts relating to other real estate and property rights of the municipality, require the approval of the provincial deputation.

3. This approval is also necessary for the acquisition of real estate and property rights by municipal councils, even though it be gratuitous, and to make leases for more than six years which require recording in the registry of property.

Municipal councils can in no manner whatsoever make gratuitous cessions of lands of the community, nor of any other class of lands or rights belonging to the municipality, except with the approval mentioned in the two foregoing paragraphs for works or services which will be of evident benefit to the municipal interests.

All contracts made by municipal councils for all kinds of services, purchases, works, sales, and leases, and in general all those which will cause expenses or receipts in the municipal funds, shall be made subject to the prescriptions of the royal decree of January 4, 1883, regarding administrative contracts.

ART. 90. The authorization of the provincial deputation is necessary in order to institute suits in the name of towns of less than four thousand inhabitants.

The resolution of the municipal council must in all cases be adopted after a favorable report of two lawyers.

No authorization or report of lawyers is necessary to utilize injunctions to retain or recover and those relating to new or old works, nor to
institute suits in which the municipal council is the defendant.

ART. 91. Whenever, in any of the cases mentioned in the foregoing
article, it is necessary to obtain the approval of the provincial deputation, it shall be the duty of the mayor to forward the data within a
period of not exceeding eight days, counted from the date of the
resolution.

ART. 92. Municipal councils in all matters which, according to this
law, are not of their exclusive competency, and in which they act by
delegation, shall be governed by the general laws and provisions relating to the same.

ART. 93. Inferior and superior courts can not admit injunctions
against administrative rulings of municipal councils and mayors in
matters of their respective competency.

ART. 94. In defined matters, such as the exclusive municipal competency, each municipal council shall enjoy all the liberty of action
compatible with obedience to the laws and the respect due private
parties.

CHAPTER II.—*Administration of towns added to a municipal district.*

ART. 95. Towns which, together with others, form a municipal district,
and have their own land, water, pasture grounds, forests, or any other
rights, exclusively their own, shall preserve the private administration
over the same.

ART. 96. For said administration they shall appoint a board, which
shall be composed of one president and two or four members, all of
whom shall be elected directly by the residents of the town and from
among them.

For towns of sixty or more residents there shall be four members,
and two for towns having a smaller number.

ART. 97. The election of the presidents and members above mentioned shall be made in accordance with the electoral law, but in one
day only, and without allowing more than eight days to elapse from
the time the municipal council was installed and which shall see to the
execution of this precept.

ART. 98. After the three or five members for the board have been
elected, the office of president shall be given the person who obtained
the highest number of votes, and should there be a tie it shall be
decided by lot.

ART. 99. The objections established by this law for municipal offices
shall also be applicable to the election of members of the board with
relation to the respective town.

ART. 100. The municipal council of the respective district shall
inspect the private administration referred to in this chapter either on
its own initiative or at the request of two or more residents of the town
interested.

ART. 101. The administration and the inspection above mentioned, as well as the duties and obligations of the board and of its members, shall be governed by the provisions of this law in all that has not been determined by this chapter.

CHAPTER III.—*Sessions and mode of procedure of municipal councils.*

ART. 102. The sessions of municipal councils shall be public, with the exception of the cases in which, for special reasons, it is resolved that they be secret; and the days and hours on which they are to be held shall be announced in the usual places.

They shall necessarily take place, under pain of nullity, in the town-halls, except in cases of force majeure.

ART. 103. The mayor and the deputy mayors, as well as the aldermen, are obliged to be present punctually at all the ordinary and extraordinary sessions, unless prevented for good reasons, which they shall prove in a proper case.

Lack of attendance shall cause a fine to be incurred for each time in accordance with the following scale:

In towns of 20,000 or more inhabitants, 15 pesetas.

In towns of over 15,000 inhabitants, 10 pesetas.

In those of more than 8,000, 5 pesetas.

In other towns, 2 pesetas.

This provision is applicable to the members of the municipal board.

ART. 104. The mayor, the deputies, and the aldermen all have the right of speech and vote in the sessions and resolutions of the municipal council.

They are equally responsible for the resolutions which they authorize with their votes without being permitted for any reason whatsoever to abstain from casting the same.

ART. 105. The municipal council shall be presided over by the mayor. In his absence the deputy shall preside, and thereafter the councilors in the order of their age.

The Governor-General and his delegate shall preside when they are present at the sessions of the municipal council, but shall not have a right to vote.

ART. 106. The mayor may call an extraordinary session when he deems fit, and he must always do so when ordered to by the delegate of the Governor-General or when it is requested by a third of the councilors.

ART. 107. In every call for an extraordinary session the business to be transacted shall be mentioned, and the municipal council can not take up any other matters at the same session.

The calls shall be made at least one day in advance, except in cases of greater urgency, and the resolutions shall be subject to ratification at the following one.

ART. 108. Every session of an ordinary character, with the exception of the days fixed in accordance with article 159 of this law, which is not called by the mayor in the manner and under the conditions prescribed in the foregoing articles or in which a question not announced in the call is treated of, shall be null and of no value, and the resolutions adopted at the same shall also be null.

ART. 109. In order to hold sessions the presence of a majority of the total number of councilors which the municipal council must have according to this law is requisite.

If at the first meeting there should not be a quorum for the adoption of resolutions, a new citation shall be made for two days later, stating the reasons therefor, and the persons present at the same may adopt resolutions, no matter what their number may be.

ART. 110. All questions which are to be resolved upon by a municipal council shall first be discussed, if necessary, and then voted upon.

Questions shall be considered as adopted which one over half of the members present at the session vote for.

In case of tie, voting shall be resumed at the next session, or at the same one, if the question is of an urgent character in the judgment of the mayor; and in case of a new tie, the latter shall cast the deciding vote.

ART. 111. Balloting shall be oral when questions relating to the councilors themselves or to members of their families within the fourth degree are not in question, being otherwise secret, the councilor interested being obliged to withdraw from the session while the matter is under discussion and being voted upon.

ART. 112. The secretary of the municipal council shall make minutes of each session, in which he shall state the names of the president and of the other councilors present, the questions treated of, and the resolutions adopted relating to the same, the result of the votes, and a list of the oral ones, should there be any.

The opinions of the minorities and their reasons shall always be included in the minutes.

The minutes shall be signed by the councilors who are present at the session, by those present when they are read, and by the secretary.

The minutes of the opening session of each municipal council shall be signed by all those who were present at the same and who know how to write, those not knowing how to sign being mentioned.

ART. 113. The book of minutes of the municipal council is a public and solemn instrument. No resolution which is not explicitly and finally included in the minutes referred to shall have any value whatsoever.

This book shall be made of the proper stamped paper, and all its sheets shall bear the rubric of the mayor and the stamp of the municipal council.

ART. 114. At the end of each month, in the capital of the island, in the seats of judicial districts, and in towns having more than four thousand inhabitants, and every three months in other towns, the secretary shall draw up an extract of the resolutions adopted by the municipal council during the same period, and after having been approved by the corporation it shall be forwarded by the mayor to the Governor-General for insertion in the Gaceta de Puerto Rico.

ART. 115. The foregoing rules shall be applied to the minutes and ses-sions of the municipal board. Their minutes shall be kept in different books from those of the municipal council, and with similar formalities, precautions, and requisites, unless otherwise ordered by this law.

ART. 116. The proceedings of examination and discussion shall never give rise to excuses to the municipal council to delay the fulfillment of the obligations imposed upon them by the laws.

CHAPTER IV.—*Administrative functions of mayors, deputies, syndics, aldermen, and ward mayors.*

ART. 117. Every resident shall have a right to request that an official certificate of the minutes, resolutions, data, and documents which he may expressly designate be issued to him which exist in the municipal archives, provided they are not of a private character, in the judgment of the corporation.

ART. 118. The mayor, who is the president of the municipal corpora-tion, bears its name and represents it in all matters, with the exception of the powers granted syndics.

ART. 119. The mayor shall—

1. Preside over sessions and direct discussions, with a right of vote.

2. Take care, under his liability, that the laws and provisions of its hierarchical superiors are fulfilled by the municipal council.

3. Communicate, in the name of the municipal council, with the necessary authorities and private parties.

ART. 120. The mayor shall also, as the chief of the municipal admin-istration—

1. Publish, execute, and order the resolutions of the municipal coun-cil complied with when they are final and there is no legal reason for their suspension; proceeding, if it is necessary, by judicial compulsion, and imposing fines, which shall in no case exceed those established by article 81, and arrest in cases of insolvency.

2. Suspend the execution of resolutions of municipal councils in the cases prescribed by articles 180 and 181 of this law.

3. Forward to the delegate of the Governor-General the resolutions of the municipal council which require the superior approval to become final, and publish, execute, and order them observed after they obtain said approval.

4. Forward statements made by municipal councils in accordance with the provisions of article 86.

5. Direct all that relates to the town and rural police, issuing for the purpose the proclamations and provisions he may deem proper in accordance with the ordinances and general regulations relating to the matter.

6. Direct and supervise the conduct of all the employees of the city

and rural police, punishing them with suspension from office and salary, not to exceed thirty days, and recommend their removal to the municipal council when they can not do so in person.

7. Exercise all the duties proper to the office of supervisor and chief of the investment of municipal funds, and of its accounting system.

8. Inspect, expedite, and direct, financially and administratively, the works, charitable institutions, and establishments of public instruction paid for by municipal funds, subject to the laws and provisions governing the matter.

9. Take care that the services relating to army equipages and lodgings and other public charges are faithfully rendered.

10. Preside over public sales and auctions for sales, leases, and municipal services in accordance to law.

11. Communicate with the Governor-General and with the authorities and corporations of the province in all questions of their governmental and administrative competency, and discharge all the special duties conferred upon them by the Governor-General or his delegate and the laws and regulations.

ART. 121. Where there is only one deputy, the mayor shall divide with him the subdistricts into which the municipal district has been divided.

Where there is more than one deputy, the subdistricts shall only be divided among the deputies.

ART. 122. The deputy mayors shall each one of them discharge in their district the functions entrusted by the law to the mayor, under the direction of the latter, as the superior chief of the municipal administration.

Ward mayors are under the orders of the deputies, and shall discharge that part of the administrative functions which the latter may delegate to them.

ART. 123. Before absenting himself from his district for more than eight days, a mayor requires permission from the delegate of the Governor-General; and if in granting the same he should not appoint a temporary mayor, the proper deputy, according to his numeration, shall substitute the former during his absence.

In cases of absences for less than eight days, it is sufficient for the mayor to summon in writing the person who is to substitute him and place the office in his charge, and to communicate this fact to the municipal council and to the delegate of the Governor-General, also in writing.

Deputies and aldermen require the permission of the municipal council to absent themselves from their district for more than eight days; but in urgent cases the mayor may authorize the absence of the deputies, informing those who are to replace them.

Even though the absence is to be less than eight days, the deputies and councilors shall communicate it to the mayor in writing.

ART. 124. Ward mayors can never absent themselves from the ward in their charge for more than twenty-four hours without permission from the mayor, who shall appoint a person to replace them during their absence.

ART. 125. Deputy mayors shall be replaced by the oldest aldermen, and the rest, according to the order established by article 105.

ART. 126. Councilors can not absent themselves without permission from the municipal council on days of ordinary or extraordinary sessions, nor for a longer period than that intervening between two ordinary sessions.

Leave of absence shall only be granted simultaneously to one-fourth of the total number of councilors.

ART. 127. Councilors shall discharge their functions within the municipal district to which they belong, without being obliged to leave the same in the discharge thereof.

CHAPTER V.—*Secretaries of municipal councils.*

ART. 128. Every municipal council shall have a secretary, to be remunerated from its funds.

The appointment shall be made by the municipal council after competition.

ART. 129. In order to be a secretary it is necessary to be a Spaniard, of age, to be in the full enjoyment of civil and political rights, and to possess an elementary education.

The following can not be regular nor temporary secretaries:

1. Councilors of the same municipal council.

2. Notaries and public clerks, as long as they discharge the functions proper to these offices.

3. Employees in office of all classes.

4. Private parties or professional people who have contracts or engagements for services with the municipal council or with a community of residents.

5. Those who, directly or indirectly, are interested in services, contracts, or in the furnishing of supplies within the municipal district on account of the latter or on account of the province.

6. Those who have an administrative or judicial question pending with the municipal council or with the establishments under its dependency or administration.

7. Debtors to the municipal funds as taxpayers.

The office of secretary is incompatible with all other municipal offices.

ART. 130. Mayors may suspend secretaries by giving to the delegate of the Governor-General a report with the necessary documents for his information and approval.

The delegate of the Governor-General, for grave reasons, may also suspend or remove secretaries of the municipal councils, reporting to the Governor-General.

From the decision of the Governor-General in the two cases mentioned, the person interested may appeal to the colonial secretary, who shall decide, hearing the council of state, without further remedy.

ART. 131. The following are the obligations of secretaries of municipal councils:

1. To take part, without the right of speech nor vote, at all the sessions of the municipal corporation, to inform the same of the correspondence and proceedings, in the manner and order prescribed by the president.

2. To draft the minutes of each session, read them at the beginning of the following one, and, after having been approved, have them transcribed faithfully in the book destined for this purpose, taking care to collect the signatures, as prescribed by article 112, and placing his full signature in the proper place.

3. To prepare the proceedings for the works of the committees and the resolution of the municipal council.

4. To make a note above his signature on each record of proceedings of the decision of the municipal council.

5. To draft the minutes of the orders and resolutions of the municipal corporation and of the committees in a proper case.

6. To prepare the proceedings, make memoranda of the resolutions, and draft the minutes of the decisions of the mayor when there is no special secretary for the purpose.

7. To issue certifications of all the official acts of the municipal corporation, and of the mayor when he has no special secretary, and to issue any other certifications which may be proper.

The latter, however, in order to be valid, require the countersignature of the mayor.

8. To direct and supervise the employés of the office of the secretary, of which he is the chief.

9. To assist boards of experts, without special remuneration, in the formation of assessments and restorations.

10. Any other duties entrusted to them by the laws or which the municipal council confers upon them within the sphere and purpose of their office.

ART. 132. Where there is no archivist, the municipal archives shall be under the custody of the secretary. He shall draw up an inventory of the papers and documents and shall complete it each year with an appendix, of which, as well as of the inventory, he shall forward a copy, with the countersignature of the mayor, to the provincial deputation.

ART. 133. In municipal councils where there is no auditor, it shall be the duty of the secretary to keep the books of receipts and expenditures of funds, authorize warrants, and enter drafts.

ART. 134. Municipal councils may impose upon their secretaries the disciplinary corrections which they may deem proper and which are within their powers for the offenses or abuses which they may commit in the discharge of their office and which do not give rise to criminal proceedings.

ART. 135. The secretaries of the municipal councils shall also be those of the mayors, but in the capital of the province and in towns of an equal or higher number of inhabitants the mayor has the power to appoint a special secretary, whose salary shall be fixed by the municipal board.

ART. 136. The secretaries of mayors, where there are such, shall, in so far as their liability is concerned, be equal to those of the respective municipal council, with the exception of the differences consequent upon their duties.

ART. 137. The secretary of the municipal council shall also be the secretary of the municipal board.

TITLE IV.

THE MUNICIPAL TREASURY.

CHAPTER I.—*Municipal budgets.*

ART. 138. The provisions of the decree of September 12th and the instructions of October 4, 1870, issued for the government of the financial administration and accounting of the colonies, are applicable to the municipal treasury.

The municipal fiscal year shall be the same as the one in force for the budgets and general accounts of the island of Puerto Rico.

ART. 139. The municipal councils shall each year draw up a budget which shall include all the expenses to be made for any reason whatsoever and the revenues to cover the same. For this purpose they shall establish from among their members one of the permanent committees mentioned in article 62.

ART. 140. The municipal councils and the boards of associates shall enjoy all the latitude of powers compatible with the tax system of the State, for the purpose of fixing the financial resources and to adopt the means preferred in each town in order to cover the services and obligations of the municipality without prejudice to the legal resources authorized by this law and by any other special one.

ART. 141. The provincial deputation has the power of revision of the decisions of municipal corporations relating to the formation or alteration of their budgets, in so far as the proportion of the expenses with the revenues is concerned, as well as the character or nature of the expenses, so that, without diminishing the discretional power of said corporations, it takes care that no expense is authorized which exceeds the cash resources, and that before any other requirement, the debits or arrears which may have gone over from one year to another be covered, as well as the obligations which may have been declared as final by the competent courts.

ART. 142. The Governor-General and his delegates have the power to intervene, in so far as necessary, in the resolutions of municipal corporations relating to the formation or alteration of their budgets to insure the observance of the laws and the compatibility of the resources of the municipal council with the revenues of the State.

ART. 143. The ordinary annual budgets shall necessarily contain the requisite sections, according to the resources of the municipality, in order to attend to and fill the obligations referred to in the first paragraph of article 78 of this law; the services established between those which, according to article 75, come under the jurisdiction of municipal councils; the expenses which, by virtue of the second paragraph of the said article 78, are clearly and finally designated in the laws as obligatory, besides the following:

1. Personnel and material of the dependencies and offices.

2. Pensions, annuities (censos), and judicial expenses, which are to be paid from municipal funds, as well as acknowledged and liquidated debts, and interest and consequences of contracts.

3. Protection of trees.

4. Preventive measures and measures for the extinguishment of fires and life-saving measures in maritime populations.

5. Subscription to the Gaceta de Puerto Rico.

6. Allotment of the municipality in the provincial assessment.

7. One section for emergencies and public calamities, not to exceed ten per cent of the budget for expenses.

8. Printing, announcements and other necessary expenses to make municipal acts public.

ART. 144. The expenses included in the municipal budgets shall be covered with the income, penalties, and means authorized by this law and other provisions in force.

ART. 145. The revenues shall be:

Rents and products accruing from property, rights or capitals which, for any reason whatsoever, belong to the municipality or to the charitable institutions or institutions of instruction and other similar ones depending on the same.

Municipal taxes or imposts on determined services, works or industries, as well as the benefit of city and rural police, and fines and indemnifications for the infraction of the municipal ordinances and police regulations.

A general assessment among all the residents and property owners in proportion to the means or powers of each one, to cover the municipal services wholly, or in the part not covered by the foregoing resources.

Taxes on articles of food, drink, and fuel.

ART. 146. For the fulfillment of the second paragraph of the foregoing article the following rules shall be observed:

1. The establishment of taxes can only be authorized on those works and services paid with the municipal funds, the benefit of which will not redound to the residents in common, but to determined persons or classes, provided the persons interested have not previously acquired

44

the same for a valuable consideration, as well as on industries which are established in public ways or on land or properties of the town, it being understood that the municipal council can not secure the monopoly nor any privilege whatsoever over said services except in so far as necessary for the public health.

2. In accordance with the provisions of the foregoing article, the establishment of taxes on the following objects may be authorized:

Benefit and provision of waters for private use.

Sewers, bathing establishments in public waters.

Rural police.

Institutions of secondary, superior, or special instruction.

Licenses for the construction of buildings.

Slaughter houses.

Public booths and chairs in squares, streets, fairs, markets, and promenades.

Rental of weights and measures.

Inspection of weights and measures or reweighing.

Interment in municipal cemeteries.

Public carriages and hearses and wagons for transportation in the interior of the towns.

Issue of certifications of acts of the municipal council or of documents existing in its archives.

Shares granted by the laws in the issue of documents of surveillance, hunting and fishing licenses, and navigation and freight transportation on rivers, and water privileges.

And other similar ones.

3. In no case can the following services be subjected to taxation:

Benefit and provision of waters for communal use.

Public lighting.

Sidewalks and paving.

Public surveillance.

Charity.

Public instruction.

Street cleaning, without prejudice to the benefits which may result.

And others of a similar character.

4. In the same manner, the establishment of taxes on the sale of spirituous or fermented drinks may also be authorized, either in establishments or fixed places, or by peddlers, carriers, or by the manufacturers or proprietors themselves; on cafés, restaurants, saloons, inns, boarding houses, and other establishments of the same character; on bathing establishments; on all kinds of public spectacles, and on permitted gambling and raffles, in so far as granted by the laws to municipal councils.

5. The taxes on the slaughterhouses shall come under the heading of consumption taxes, should there be any, and can not altogether exceed twenty-five per cent, in accordance with the second paragraph, rule 1, article 151; where there is no consumption tax on meats, there

can only be imposed by way of slaughter tax an amount which shall never exceed ten per cent of the value of the head of cattle.

6. The taxes mentioned in rule 4 of this article, with the exception of those relating to bathing establishments, public spectacles, gambling, and raffles, shall not be authorized when any consumption taxes exist, but the establishments mentioned may at any rate be subjected to a special tax on account of surveillance, which shall not exceed five per cent of the amount they pay as a direct tax.

7. The taxes on industries which are carried on in public roads shall not exist jointly with the general assessment, without prejudice to which the quotas which correspond for this reason to the manufacturers may be charged with five per cent by reason of rental or use of the road.

8. The quotas imposed on the industries mentioned in this law, which are included in the schedules of the industrial, commercial, and professional tax, shall not exceed twenty-five per cent of the amount indicated in the latter; and

9. The payment of fines and indemnifications shall be made in the special paper which the treasury shall issue for the case, and which it shall deliver to the municipal councils who request it, charging on the same by reason of the stamp a tax not exceeding ten per cent of its nominal value.

ART. 146. The creation of any of the taxes mentioned shall be resolved upon by the municipal councils in union with the board of associates, the record of proceedings being forwarded through the mayor to the delegates of the governor, who shall transmit it, after a report, to the Governor-General for the proper resolution, according to article 142.

The Governor-General shall forward said record of proceedings to the provincial deputation for the purposes of article 141.

ART. 148. In order that the general assessment referred to in the third paragraph of article 145 may be authorized, the municipal council shall institute proceedings in accordance with the following rules:

1. The assessment shall be extended to the following persons for all the utilities they may have in the district, irrespective of their nature:

First. To the residents of the municipal district.

Second. To owners living in other towns who, according to article 27, are considered residents.

Third. To those who, according to the same article, have the character and are considered as owners.

Fourth. To farmers, lessees, or coproprietors of agricultural estates who do not reside in the district.

The profits accruing from pensions, interest on capitals, salaries, or state revenues in the town where they reside shall be imputed to their possessors.

Persons who have been declared paupers, those taken care of in charitable institutions, and members of the army and navy are exempted from the assessment.

2. In order to fix the income of each taxpayer, the following bases shall be observed:

First. On owners of city property there shall be assessed as taxable income the amount of the rents they receive or may hereafter receive for this purpose, taking into consideration the nature and conditions of the estates, if they are occupied by them personally, or by others who do not pay rent.

Second. Owners who cultivate agricultural estates, or in the proper case the farmers, lessees, or coproprietors, shall be assessed a sum amounting to one and a half times the amount of the rent produced by the estate, or which it might hereafter produce, according to the average rents of the town, should said estate be rented.

Third. When the owners of estates, be they either rural or town, are not residents of the district, the assessment shall be reduced by one-fifth of the sum which, according to the foregoing bases, it should have amounted to.

Fourth. To those who receive salaries, pensions, annuities (censos), or interests of any class or from any source, the amount of these sums shall be assessed as net income.

Fifth. Persons included in the industrial, commercial, and professional tax shall be assessed the net profit assessable in proportion to the quota they pay by reason thereof, which shall not be less than five nor exceed twenty times the amount of said quota, in accordance with the scales approved for each class.

Sixth. Day-laborers and journeymen, and in general all those who live upon a fortuitous salary, shall be assessed upon a third part of the sum which, according to the customs of each locality, their income may reach during the year, on an average.

Seventh. When it is not possible to ascertain the income of any resident, the assessment shall be made without prejudice to the provisions of article 27 and rule 3 of this article, taking into consideration the external marks of wealth, such as the value of the furniture, rental of the house, number of servants, and other similar ones.

Eighth. From the assessed income of each resident or property holder, there shall be deducted in every case the amount of the direct tax he pays the State.

3. The determination of the taxable income shall be made by the taxpayers themselves, divided into sections in the manner prescribed by chapter 3, title 2, of this law.

Each section shall draw up a statement, including the profits of all its members, specifying, in so far as possible, the nature and number of the objects which produce the same.

ART. 149. After the proceedings have been instituted in the manner stated, the municipal council shall issue the proper resolution, without prejudice to the powers appertaining to the provincial deputation and to the Governor-General, in accordance with this law.

ART. 150. After the assessment has been approved its collection shall be proceeded with, the following rules being observed:

1. The members of each section of taxpayers, proceeding as syndics and meeting with the municipal council, shall examine and compare the statements of income, deciding the complaints which may arise and fixing the total amount assessable.

The board shall assess the amount corresponding to each section either by so much per cent in proportion to the total appraised income or by fixed classes.

2. The syndics of each section shall make and communicate the assessment to the members of the same. The municipal council shall decide the complaints which this assessment may cause.

3. All the operations of appraisement and assessment shall be published in the ordinary manner, and shall furthermore be communicated in the office of the secretary of the municipal council to every person interested who requests it.

4. From the decisions of the municipal council and of the board of appraisement an appeal lies to the provincial deputation. The appeal must be instituted within the fifteen days following the publication, and it shall not hinder the payment of the quota assessed until a definite resolution is reached.

These complaints, as well as those which may be brought on account of the work of each section, must be based on concrete, precise, and determined facts, adducing the proofs necessary for their justification.

5. The assessment shall include an increase, not to exceed six per cent of the total quota, for expenses of distribution, collection, and quotas which can not be collected.

Taxpayers who pay their quotas every three months, six months, or every year in advance into the treasuries of the respective municipalities are exempted from the payment of this increase, and in the second and third cases they shall be credited so much per cent per annum, which may be fixed by reason of the advanced payment.

6. Owners and farmers, lessees, coproprietors, or tenants shall arrange by means of private contracts the proportion to be paid by each one of the quota assessed the latter, on the estates, and the manner and time of reimbursing each other for this quota.

ART. 151. For the fulfillment of the fourth paragraph of article 145, proceedings shall be instituted, the following rules being observed:

1. The municipal council and the associates united in a board shall determine the subjects which are to be the object of the consumption tax, as well as the schedules which are to govern its collection and the manner of doing so.

The schedules shall in no case exceed twenty-five per cent of the average of the article in the respective locality, according to its class.

2. The tax can only be placed upon the articles of food or of drink which are consumed in each town. Any other tax on the same which

might embarrass traffic, circulation, and sale, no matter under what name it may be desired to establish the same, is absolutely prohibited.

3. In towns where customs houses are established foreign articles, after being nationalized by the payment of the customs duties, may be subjected to the municipal consumption tax within the prescriptions of this law, and on the value which they have in the market, by deducting the amount of said customs duties.

ART. 152. After the consumption tax on any of the provisions approved has been established the municipal council shall fix the individual quotas and their collection. The assessment shall include an increase not to exceed six per cent of the total quota for the expenses of distribution, collection, and quotas that can not be collected.

Against the decision of the municipal council and the board of associates an appeal lies in the shape and manner prescribed by rule 4 of article 150.

ART. 153. At the end of the fiscal year the open credits which have not been invested during the course of the same are annulled.

During the period of extension the operations of collection of the budget incomes shall be concluded, as well as those for the liquidation and payment of the services effected during the year. The balances remaining after this period shall be the subject of an additional budget, after the consequent liquidations which shall be concluded during the following month.

ART. 154. When, in order to cover unforeseen expenses, satisfy some debt, or for any other important object not determined in the ordinary budget, the resources included in the same are not sufficient, the municipal councils shall draw up an extraordinary budget in the same manner and with the same procedure fixed for the ordinary ones.

ART. 155. The debts of towns which are not secured by pledges or mortgages can not be judicially demanded of municipal councils.

When any town is sentenced to the payment of a sum, the municipal council, in the period of ten days after the sentence has been carried out, shall draw up an extraordinary budget, unless the creditor agrees to postpone the collection, in order to permit the entry in the ordinary following budgets, of the sums necessary for the payment of the principal and interest stipulated.

ART. 156. If the resources at the disposal of a town are not sufficient to cover its debts, or the municipal council does not consider it possible to collect the increased quotas imposed upon the residents, and the creditors are not satisfied with the means offered them to liquidate their debts, the proceedings shall be forwarded to the provincial deputation, which shall order what is proper so that the payments can be made without prejudice to the competency of the superior and ordinary inferior courts to decide regarding the legality and preference of the credits.

ART. 157. Resources originating from means of a fortuitous and transitory character can not be applied to the payment and fulfillment of permanent services or obligations.

ART. 158. The project of the budget, either ordinary, additional, or extraordinary, with the report of the syndic, shall be exhibited to the public in the office of the secretary of the municipal council for the period of fifteen days from the date on which the announcement is made in the ordinary form.

ART. 159. The municipal council shall draw up the budget, which shall be approved by the municipal board without prejudice to the provisions of article 162.

ART. 160. The municipal boards shall meet, after a personal citation and announcement, at the times and in the manner prescribed by article 71.'

ART. 161. In order to adopt resolutions, the vote of an absolute majority of the total number of members who compose the board is necessary. If this number does not meet at the first session a new call shall be issued for eight days later, at which a majority of those present may adopt resolutions.

In towns of less than eight hundred inhabitants the vote of one over half of those present shall form a quorum, if they reach at least the fourth part of the total number of residents who have a right to compose the board. In case this number should not assemble, the provisions of the foregoing paragraph shall be observed.

ART. 162. The resolutions of the board relating to the budgets may be appealed from to the Governor-General by the persons who are injured thereby, when any provisions of the law are infringed by the same, but only in so far as the infraction is concerned.

The governor shall decide, without loss of time, first hearing the council of administration.

ART. 163. The mayor may authorize the execution, making a report to the provincial deputation and to the delegate of the Governor-General, without prejudice to the subsequent appeals which may be proper according to this law, of the budgets drawn up to attend to the sanitary requirements of absolute urgency, in time of public calamity, and others of a peremptory character, when the amount does not exceed two pesetas and fifty céntimos for each resident, nor one-third of the ordinary budget.

ART. 164. In order to effect the collection, the judicial means regarding direct and indirect taxpayers issued in favor of the treasury shall be applicable.

CHAPTER II.—*Collection, distribution, and accounting of municipal funds.*

ART. 165. The collection and administration of the municipal funds are in charge of the respective municipal councils, and shall take place through its agents and delegates.

4080——4

ART. 166. The distribution and investment of the funds shall be resolved upon every month by the municipal council, subject to the budgets.

ART. 167. Payments shall be ordered by the mayor.

The supervision shall be in charge of the auditor, where there is one, and in his absence the office shall be filled by an alderman elected by the municipal council.

In towns the budget of expenses of which is not under one hundred thousand pesetas there shall be an auditor of municipal funds appointed by the municipal council from among the persons who possess the qualifications determined by special regulations.

The same regulations shall prescribe all that refers to the classes and salaries of said officials.

The removal of municipal auditors who are appointed in accordance with its provisions shall appertain to the municipal councils, but it shall not be ordered, except for serious reasons and after proceedings. The persons interested may appeal from the decision to the delegate of the Governor, who shall decide, hearing the provincial committee.

ART. 168. The municipal councils shall appoint and freely remove the treasurers and agents for the collection of all the revenues and means of the municipality.

The same corporations shall also fix the remuneration which said employees are to enjoy and the guarantees they are to give.

If there should not be in the town any person wishing to take charge of the custody of funds, the office of depositary shall be declared as appertaining to the council and obligatory, but it shall not require the giving of a guarantee, and the expenses which may arise shall be for the account of the municipality.

ART. 169. The agents for the municipal collection are liable to the municipal council, and the latter is civilly liable to the municipality in case of negligence or omission duly proven without prejudice to the rights which may be exercised against the agents.

ART. 170. All the municipal funds shall necessarily be deposited in the treasury of the municipal council, the three keys of which shall be in the custody of the depositary, the comptroller, and the supervisor.

ART. 171. The auditor or supervising councilor, assisted if necessary by the secretary and other clerks of the municipal council, shall draw up the accounts of each term at the proper time, which shall be submitted, with the documents justifying them, to the municipal council after having been audited by the syndic.

ART. 172. After the accounts have been definitely fixed by the municipal council they shall be forwarded, with a report of the syndic and the documents justifying them, for auditing and revision to the municipal board.

The latter, on the first working day of the second quarter of the fiscal year, shall assemble in the building of the municipal council, under the presidency of the mayor, with the presence of the secretary, and shall appoint a committee from its members, who, after examining the accounts, shall make a report within a period not to exceed fifteen days. During the fifteen days preceding the assembly, the accounts shall be exhibited in the office of the secretary, and any resident may examine them and put his observations in writing, which shall be communicated to the board.

ART. 173. The sessions which the board dedicates to the discussion of the report of the committee shall be presided over by a member elected by the same.

ART. 174. After the accounts have been examined and discussed and all the proceedings instituted and the data procured which may be considered necessary by the board, it shall assemble to resolve upon and adopt its definite decision by a vote of the absolute majority.

This report shall be subscribed by all those present, no matter what their private opinion may be, which they may, however, record by means of a written vote, the original of which shall be attached to the record of proceedings, this fact being stated in the minutes.

ART. 175. The municipal board shall assemble in the first fifteen days of February, in order to revise and audit the accounts of the previous fiscal year in the manner prescribed by the foregoing articles.

ART. 176. The annual accounts of the mayors, comprising the receipts and ordinary and extraordinary expenditures, shall be published in the locality, revised and audited in view of the objections, by the delegate of the region, hearing the persons responsible regarding the objections, and definitely approved or disapproved by the provincial deputation.

ART. 177. The provincial deputation may declare without further appeal the administrative liabilities which may be proper, with the exception of those which come under the jurisdiction of the ordinary courts.

ART. 178. The municipal council shall publish, at the beginning of each quarter, a statement of the collection and investment of its funds during the preceding one.

In public works which may be made by administration, there shall be published every week a memorandum of the expenses incurred, detailing the amount paid for wages, material, traders, contractors, site of the work, and other similar circumstances.

In the office of the secretary there shall be exhibited all the year round, on working days and during office hours, to any resident, and specially to the associate members of the municipal boards, the original documents and accounts, from which the municipal council shall permit memoranda to be made, as well as copies of the same.

Accounts which involve more than one hundred thousand pesetas shall be printed in an abstract, which shall include the report of the board and the remarks of the municipal council, which shall be sold to the public.

ART. 179. The municipal councils shall forward to the delegate of the region a full copy, certified by the secretary, with the counter signature of the mayor, as well as copies of the budgets and accounts definitely approved, with the literal minutes of the municipal board.

TITLE V.

APPEALS AND LIABILITIES ARISING FROM THE ACTS OF MUNICIPAL COUNCILS.

CHAPTER I.—*Appeals from the decisions of municipal councils.*

ART. 180. Without prejudice to the provisions of article 120, the mayor is obliged to suspend in person or at the instance of any resident of the town, the execution of decisions of the municipal council in the following cases:

1. When questions are involved which, according to this law and other special ones do not come under the jurisdiction of the municipal council.

2. For delinquency.

The reasons for the suspension shall be given in either case, stating concretely and precisely the legal provisions on which it is based.

In cases of incompetency, want of jurisdiction, infraction of the law, prejudice of the general interests, or danger to public order, the mayor shall suspend the decisions of the municipal council, reporting thereon to the delegate of the Governor for the proper resolution.

ART. 181. The mayor shall also suspend the execution of the decisions referred to in the first paragraph of the foregoing article when thereby the civil rights of a third person might be damaged, be he a resident or not of the municipal district.

The suspension in such case shall only be granted when requested by the person interested, complaining at the same time against the decision.

ART. 182. The complaint authorized by the foregoing article shall be brought before the mayor within a period of thirty days, counted from the date of the publication of the decision.

The mayor, under his personal liability, shall forward the appeal with his report within the period of eight days to the Governor-General, who shall decide, hearing the provincial committee.

ART. 183. Persons who consider themselves damaged in their civil rights by the decisions of the municipal councils, even though their execution has been suspended or not suspended in virtue of the provisions of the foregoing articles, may object to the same by means of a complaint made to the judge or court of competent jurisdiction, according to what may be provided by the laws, taking into consideration the nature of the question.

The judge or court taking cognizance of the matter may suspend the execution of the decision appealed from at the petition of the person interested, by means of a preliminary ruling, if it has not already been suspended, according to the provisions of article 181, when in his judgment it is proper and convenient in order to avoid a grave and irreparable damage.

In order to make this complaint a period of thirty days is granted after the notification of the decision or the communication of the suspension in a proper case, and if said period has elapsed without any complaint having been made, this suspension is raised as of course and the decision adopted.

ART. 184. If any decision has been suspended or appealed from by virtue of the provisions of the foregoing articles, the mayor shall forward the data to the delegate of the Governor-General within the period of eight days, for the proper ends.

In all cases in which the governmental suspension has been ordered by reason of delinquency, the delegate shall immediately forward the question for the information of the ordinary court.

ART. 185. If the reason for the suspension was that the resolution related to questions absolutely foreign to the municipal jurisdiction, or for having infringed the laws, the matter shall be forwarded to the provincial deputation for its confirmation or revocation.

ART. 186. The delegates of the Governor-General may suspend the resolutions of municipal corporations when they extend over the limit of their jurisdiction, forwarding the data at once to the Governor-General for his decision.

CHAPTER II.—*Dependency and liability of councilors and their agents.*

ART. 187. The Governor-General of the Island of Puerto Rico is the superior chief of the municipal councils of the province.

The municipal councils are also subordinate to the provincial deputation in so far as determined by the laws.

ART. 188. The municipal councils, mayors and councilors incur liability:

1. For a manifest infraction of the law in their acts or resolutions, either making use of powers to which they have no right or abusing their own.

2. For disobedience or disrespect to their hierarchical superiors.

3. For negligence or omission which may result in damage to the interests or services which are under their custody.

ART. 189. The liability shall be demandable before the administration or before the courts, according to the nature of the action or omission which gave rise thereto, and shall only be extended to the members who took part in the same.

ART. 190. Without prejudice to the provisions of articles 52 and 54, regarding mayors and deputies, when the latter or the aldermen of a municipal council are guilty of acts or omissions administratively punishable, they shall incur, according to the cases, the penalties of warning, reprimand, fine, or suspension.

ART. 191. A warning is proper in cases of error, omission, or slight negligence, which is not repeated and if the damage caused thereby can be easily repaired.

Reprimands are proper in cases of second offenses, already corrected, and in cases of extra limitation of power, and abuse of faculties, and negligence, the consequences of which are not irreparable or serious.

A fine is proper, provided the laws and general provisions in accordance to the same fix it, and in cases of repetitions of offences, punished with reprimands, and in extra limitations, abuse of authority, serious negligence or disobedience, which do not require suspension nor produce criminal liability.

ART. 192. The delegates of the Governor-General may warn, reprimand, fine, and suspend from office the mayors, deputy mayors, and aldermen who compose the municipal corporations when they go beyond the limit of their municipal competency.

ART. 193. The maximum of the quota of the fines which the delegate of the Governor-General may impose on mayors, deputy mayors, and aldermen for the offences which they respectively commit, and according to the provisions of the present law, shall be in proportion to the number of councilors of each town, as follows:

Number of councilors.	Mayors.	Aldermen.
	Pesetas.	Pesetas.
5 to 7	50	10
8 to 10	75	12
11 to 14	100	25
15 to 18	125	40
19 to 21	150	50

ART. 194. For the imposition and collection of fines the following rules shall be observed:

1. No fine shall be imposed without a resolution in writing stating the reasons therefor.

2. The ruling shall be communicated in writing to the person fined, and a receipt shall be issued him on its payment.

3. The fines and penalties shall be collected in the corresponding stamped paper.

4. The fines must necessarily be paid from the personal funds of the persons fined.

5. The fines shall be extended to all the members of the municipal council who, according to this law, are responsible for the act or the resolution which gave rise thereto.

ART. 195. For the payment of all fines a period shall be granted in proportion to the amount of the same, and which shall not be less than ten days nor more than twenty, at the expiration of which judicial compulsion against the delinquent persons is proper. The delinquency shall be fined by not more than five per cent daily of the total amount of the fine, without ever exceeding double the amount of the latter.

ART. 196. The person interested may complain against the imposition of a fine to the same delegate of the Governor-General, requesting that it be appealed from, with the reasons which justify it.

Against a ruling confirming the fine imposed an appeal lies on account of an error of form to the court of competent jurisdiction in administrative litigation of the province, subject to the laws in force.

After the fine has been definitely delared as improper, the return of the amount thereof to the person interested shall be ordered.

ART. 197. No writs of attachments for the collection of fines shall be administratively issued.

When the persons fined do not pay the fine notwithstanding the judicial compulsion, the delegate of the Governor-General shall address a communication to the judge of first instance of the judicial district, stating the cause which gave rise to the imposition of the fine and the amount and liquidation of the latter, and requesting his authority to enforce the same.

The judge shall proceed to the collection of the fine through the proceedings of judicial compulsion.

ART. 198. The Governor-General may freely suspend mayors.

ART. 199. He may also suspend deputy mayors and aldermen when they commit serious acts of extra limitation of a political character, and especially in the following cases:

1. To have given publicity to the act.
2. For inciting other municipal councils to commit the same.
3. For causing a disturbance of the public order.

He may also order the suspension when the deputies and aldermen commit serious acts of disobedience, insisting therein after having been reprimanded and fined.

ART. 200. The suspension of deputies and aldermen shall not exceed four months.

If this period has elapsed without the institution of a suit or administrative removal having been ordered, the persons suspended shall return to the discharge of their functions, the persons who took their place discontinuing the same.

ART. 201. The Governor-General shall forward to the colonial department the records of proceedings of suspension by the first mail after they have been ordered.

When the colonial secretary believes that the suspension of mayors, deputies, aldermen, and syndics is not proper, he shall immediately raise the same, annulling the resolution of the Governor.

In a contrary case the record of proceedings shall be forwarded to the council of state, which, after hearing his opinion, shall decide what may be proper.

In cases of urgency, it shall decide alone without requiring such procedure.

The resolution shall always state the reasons therefor and shall be published in the gazettes of Madrid and Puerto Rico.

If the Government does not agree with the opinion of the council of state, the report of the latter body shall be published at the same time and in the same manner as the resolution of the Government.

ART. 202. The Governor-General may administratively remove mayors, deputy mayors, and aldermen, in the cases determined by law.

In order to do so, it must previously and necessarily hear the council of administration.

Against this resolution a litigative administrative appeal lies.

ART. 203. In case criminal liability exists, the Governor-General shall forward the record to the court of first instance of the judicial district to which the municipal council of which said persons are members belongs.

The judges and courts shall apply in these cases the provisions of the penal code.

ART. 204. After the suspension has been raised in accordance with article 201, or the persons interested have been absolved from criminal responsibility, they shall retake possession of their offices, if during the proceedings it would not have been proper for them to have discontinued therein in accordance with article 45, the provisions of article 200 being observed with regard to them.

ART. 205. Councilors judicially or administratively removed shall be disqualified to discharge similar functions again for six years at least.

ART. 206. The vacancies which occur in the municipal council on account of legal suspension and removal shall be filled in the manner prescribed by article 46.

ART. 207. The suspension and removal of ward mayors appertains exclusively to mayors.

The suspension shall not exceed fifteen days; the fines which may be imposed upon the same shall be reduced to half of those prescribed for councilors.

The criminal liability which they may incur by reason of their acts shall be enforced before the judge of first instance, according to the provisions of article 203.

The raising of the suspension or the judicial absolution in a proper case does not give them a right but only qualifies them again to be reinstated in office.

ART. 208. All the employees and agents of the municipal council appointed and paid by the same shall obey its orders and are administratively liable to the same in accordance with this law, and judicially to the courts for the crimes and offenses which they may commit.

ART. 209. Besides the administrative appeals established by this

law, any resident or property owner of the town has a right of action
to the courts of justice in order to denounce and criminally prosecute
mayors, deputy mayors, or aldermen and associates, whenever in the
establishment, distribution, and collection of taxes and imposts they
have been guilty of fraud or of illegal exactions, and more especially
in the following cases:

1. If any of the councilors or associates, during the year they are
such, pay a quota lower by way of assessment, tax, or license, compared
with the year preceding the discharge of their office, the total amount
assessable being equal or higher, unless they prove that their wealth
has diminished sufficiently to justify such reduction.

2. When the total products of the assessments and taxes distributed
exceed the amount mentioned in the budget and six per cent extra
authorized by rule 5 of article 150 of this law.

3. When the quotas determined by the means are higher than the law
allows.

4. Whenever any kind of imposts not included in the budget are
established and collected.

The courts of justice, after the act has been proved, and without
prejudice to the provisions of the penal code, shall make the following
declarations:

First case. Imposition of a double quota upon the guilty parties.

Second and third cases. Annulment of the assessment, in so far as it
exceeds the amount authorized, and return of the taxes collected, with
a fine equal to the excess conjointly imposed upon the guilty councilors
and associates.

Fourth case. Annulment of the tax imposed, and return of the
amounts collected, with a fine equal to their value, demanded in the
manner mentioned in the foregoing case.

ART. 210. Every member of a municipal corporation who may have
made a ruling or voted for a resolution injurious to the rights of private
parties shall be liable for indemnification or for restitution to the
persons prejudiced before the courts which, according to the cases, are
of competent jurisdiction, during the time said liability is not extin-
guished according to ordinary legal rules.

TITLE VI.

POLITICAL GOVERNMENT OF MUNICIPAL DISTRICTS.

FIRST AND LAST CHAPTER.

ART. 211. Mayors, besides the administrative functions which appertain to them as executors of the resolutions of municipal councils, have
the representation and delegation of the government, and in this character they shall discharge all the duties entrusted to them by the laws,
working under the direction of the Governor-General, as said laws may

determine, in all that refers to the publication and execution of the laws and general provisions of the government or of the Governor-General and provincial deputation, as well as in all that refers to public order and to the other functions entrusted to them.

ART. 212. In all that relates to the political government of the municipal district the authority, duties, and liability of the mayor are independent of the respective municipal council.

ART. 213. Deputy mayors, in their respective sections, shall always act by delegation and under the direction of the mayor as the representatives of the government in the same manner as the mayor does in the municipal district.

ART. 214. Ward mayors, in their respective wards, exercise the functions of the political government when, in accordance to law, they are delegated thereto by the mayors or deputy mayors, in all cases complying with the provisions of the former and of the delegate of the governor.

ART. 215. The Governor-General and the colonial secretary, in the respective cases, exercise the high inspection over all the services of the island, no matter in what shape they may be rendered, in accordance with the powers inherent to the sovereignty reserved by the laws to the government of the nation.

ADDITIONAL PROVISIONS.

1. All prior laws and provisions relating to the municipal government of the island of Puerto Rico are hereby repealed.

2. The laws, decrees, royal orders, and regulations in force in the Peninsula which decide special points of municipal administration, or which are a complement or development unforeseen in this law, shall govern as suppletory legislation, in so far as they may be applied to the special case in question, and in the lack of a legal precept or administrative provision issued to the contrary for the island of Puerto Rico.

3. The Government shall issue, in accordance with this law, the provisions necessary for its execution.

Madrid, December 31st, 1896.

Approved by Her Majesty.

CASTELLANO.

O

www.ingramcontent.com/pod-product-compliance
Lightning Source LLC
Chambersburg PA
CBHW021542270326
41930CB00008B/1336